the **weight**
of a
**cherry
blossom**

Shruti Buddhavarapu is a poet, writer and editor currently living in New Delhi. She has a double master's from Jawaharlal Nehru University and the University of British Columbia. She is fascinated with politics, pop culture and how seamlessly one bleeds into the other. She is also a researcher with an interest in the rhetoric of health and medicine. Her first book, *Mother Steals a Bicycle and Other Stories,* co-authored with Salai Selvam, was published in 2019.

the weight of a cherry blossom

of a

by SHRUTI BUDDHAVARAPU

Published by
Rupa Publications India Pvt. Ltd 2019
7/16, Ansari Road, Daryaganj
New Delhi 110002

Sales centres:
Allahabad Bengaluru Chennai
Hyderabad Jaipur Kathmandu
Kolkata Mumbai

Copyright © Shruti Buddhavarapu 2019

Illustrations by Veda Aggarwal and Prutha Kulkarni

All rights reserved.

No part of this publication may be reproduced, transmitted,
or stored in a retrieval system, in any form or by any means,
electronic, mechanical, photocopying, recording or otherwise,
without the prior permission of the publisher.

The views and opinions expressed in this book are the author's own and the facts
are as reported by him/her which have been verified to the extent possible, and
the publishers are not in any way liable for the same.

ISBN: 978-93-5333-699-8

First impression 2019

10 9 8 7 6 5 4 3 2 1

The moral right of the author has been asserted.

Printed by HT Media Ltd, Gr. Noida

This book is sold subject to the condition that it shall not,
by way of trade or otherwise, be lent, resold, hired out, or otherwise
circulated, without the publisher's prior consent, in any form
of binding or cover other than that in which it is published.

I'm doing badly, I'm doing well; whichever you prefer.

—*Franz Kafka*

*To my parents, who gave me the world,
and to Dina, who made me see it.*

Contents

Prologue / xiii

I: Weight
Introduction / 3
Hunger / 8
Story / 26
Love / 35
Reading / 50
Flesh / 65
Death / 103

II: Weightlessness
Introduction / 119
Travel / 127
Loneliness / 140
Dating / 152
Planting / 164

Acknowledgements / 187

Weight

Stories and incidents that both make my centre of gravity strong, and things that weigh me/a woman down. Chronic illness and how it is processed by society, friends and family. Processing life through literal weight and also the emotional weight of conditioning to expect true love, companionship, romanticized notions of success, and the promise of good health.

Weightlessness

Learning to let go, being buoyed, rootless. Finding meaning in the rootlessness. Finding companionship in community. Unlearning expectations from self/life in terms of marriage or kids. Rooting a sense of belonging and home through objects and items instead. Finding power in other women and the spaces we nurture and build. Approaching love and dating with self-assuredness, even if not exactly confidence.

Prologue

In 2018, I turned thirty. I was living in Chennai, working as an editor in a publishing house, and had, by this point, been living by myself for a good part of the decade. Whether I was actually asked or not, I'd declare to just about anyone how happy I was to throw my twenties to the curb, uncaring of how they'd be remembered later. 'This is going to be the best decade of my life,' I'd say. Three months after turning thirty, just at the corner of the year's turning, I found myself curled up in my parents' house, waking up in the middle of the night (yet again) in a bout of panic, disoriented and, for a few seconds, incapable of telling where I was.

I'd go on to have a near-mental-breakdown, leave the job I had put so much into and move back in with family in Delhi to sift through and gather what parts of me were truly mine. I was split like a pea pod, snapped open, my anxieties infusing into the air around me. I don't remember the first two weeks of moving back home, except that they seemed unreal, and like I was elsewhere all the time. And because anxiety has a habit of spreading itself into whatever dimensions it is indulged in, and because my family gave me the world, it expanded, swelled, bloated and distended into every nook and cranny, until I found that everything at home was awash with my afflictions, and—after months, and possibly years, of me disciplining it into behaving—it finally, and thus fully, peaked in both might and fury.

It's a phrase I seem to use often—'I found myself in…' I'm often suddenly 'finding myself in' this or that, as if I merely stumble into the emotional situations I am in. I seem to indicate that my depressive or anxious episodes crept up on me, that I couldn't sense them coming before they were, in fact, there in their full-blown, evolved-Pokemon glory. As if they hadn't politely knocked every now and then, for years, hoping for a chat, as if all of this hadn't been building up, as if they 'hadn't sent me curt telegrams from the battle zone inside before seeming to disappear altogether. As if I hadn't thought to myself it was a situation well handled, again. But there they all were, having grown into as much of an adult as I was, ensuring they would be addressed, ensuring rapture… ensuring rupture.

After years of dealing with anxiety and high-functioning depressive symptoms, I still can't really articulate what it is that I feel during any of these episodes.

My father is a journalist, and I spent some time as a child in the printing press, smelling fresh ink evaporating off the damp newsprint. I'd sit next to him on weekends with my cartoon supplements, each of us individually poring over newspapers. Sometimes, the print would run heavy on these pages, making the images look like they were superimposed on each other (they are, but you don't want it to show), just that little bit out of order. You'd have one Garfield in a washed-out panel, more red than orange, and another Garfield right on top, with a more-blue-than-orange border around him like a halo. This happens almost always due to a misalignment of printing plates. Since each newsprint would pass through the C, M, Y, K plates individually, if even one of the plates was slightly out of alignment, the image on the final print would appear to separate, causing you to squint at this non-homogenous visual brought to you by a curdling of printing plates.

I wonder if that is not an accurate analogy for what often happens to me. My layers don't sit accurately on each other. My mind and body are slightly out of alignment for the most part, until the rare day that they align themselves and everything clicks, only to *find myself* aching in the places I didn't even know hurt.

I often wonder about the timing of my mental unravelling. Why in Delhi? Why at this exact moment and not the one before it, or the one after? How did I keep it together long enough to just make the flight home? How is it that I exerted any control over my mind and body at all, and with what raw materials did I manage to create a force shield around me right until the very end? I read somewhere that it's only when you move into a better situation that the mind allows itself to collapse gloriously, no longer wired by fear. I can only guess that when I finally registered that I was safe enough to *collapse* amongst loved ones, did I dissolve. Soaking overnight in this bodily trauma, blooming into a spindly mass of neuroses, fearful of being alone again, and baffled at the person who seemed to have done it so confidently for a decade before this.

And, somehow, in all of this, I manage to steal time to reach out to the possibility of love. I've only just moved back to Delhi, and by this time it's a habit, this online recce. Maybe now, I think (this is not the same as hope). Maybe. But nothing has changed. It's always the same people, floating on the same few apps, looking for the same things they did years ago when you had matched with them. I go through the motions, my thumb swiping over pictures of men so quickly that their faces and names don't even register any more. Eventually, they mesh into one personality—a colloid of leather jackets, manicured stubbles and sunglasses, with alcohol in one hand, a dog in the other, jumping out of an airplane in a foreign country, and somehow always a VP at JP Morgan. There are maybe two or three days' worth of conversation with the people I match with. By now, I know that sudden intimacy might well be genuine but it is unsustainable. No matter how life-changing the conversation, it will fizzle out and end. It has to. Something has to relieve that pressure before it implodes on itself and someone burns out before the other. The relentless brightness of sudden and torrential intimacy is painful. *(You learn over the years that, though enjoyable, it's not something you necessarily want.)* I delete the apps all over again. It is almost comical, this going to sea to fish in my rickety boat during a thunderstorm. I know I will find nothing there, but perhaps I do it to confirm this to myself. I am aware, somewhere at the back of my mind, that this is an empty performance, there are no proofs in self-fulfilling prophecies. This illusion of choice, that there is a sea of eligible partners for you in the first place, and that that sea is yours for the taking.

I keep thinking love will save me. But it always asks me to set my papers in order first. Be better, feel better, turn up with more enthusiasm, make dates, make it to dates, be chill, be open to love but also don't *actively* want it.

A month from the incident, and after being injected (twice a week) into mental wakefulness, I head back to Chennai to wrap up what I had so abruptly had to abandon. It is clear that the life I have built so determinedly, all by myself, cannot go on. I want to start piecing myself back together in the privilege of an emotional support system.

The two nights I spend in Chennai packing up my things are, like I had feared, sleepless and peaceless. It is clear that my brain associates my room there with a particular blend of panic and despair, which I used to dread and then sleep with every night for months. But packing is a bodily reflex, a habit curated over years, and so I fit my life, once again, into six bags and a courier receipt, and head home. And perhaps there's some release in closure, perhaps the deficiencies are evening out, or maybe whoever is controlling my Sims character has tweaked my traits to feel spurts of confidence again. But on the flight back home, I feel like I've woken up to the right moment at the right time. I see my father's half-open mouth as he sleeps on the next seat, and for the first time in a long time, I don't think of his eventual death. My mind grazes over what I'm going back to, what from, and for the first time in a long time, I don't feel shameful about needing people. For the first time in a long time, I keep my eyes closed during turbulence (*the plane will survive just fine without me being on high-alert; disasters are out of my control*) and I feel, for a moment, weightless. Careening homewards in a big metal tube at 850 kmph, and yet, somehow, so very still at last.

I
Weight

grounding / sinking / anchoring / drowning
pulling down
giving heft

Introduction

Only too late in the game did I discover that my life had a clear, overarching theme to it. As a literature postgraduate, and lifelong reader and consumer of stories, it is a tad embarrassing that it took me this long to realize what it was.

All through my growing-up years, and even now, two of my recurring nightmares have involved errant elevators and deep space. Although the context and tone of these dreams change, the basic principle is always the same. During the course of a dream, I suddenly find myself in an elevator and press a button. Then, I watch in horror as the elevator either steadily skips the floor I mean to get off at, or jerks noisily in the opposite direction—shooting up when I want to go down, plummeting into an abyss when I want to go up.

At other times, I find myself slowly floating up and out of whatever dream situation I'm in. I'll be talking to a long-lost friend one second, only to find myself being plucked off the surface of the Earth in the next. I steadily float above people, buildings, skyscrapers, clouds, the stratosphere, to a point so far out that Earth is a distant, shiny speck. I bob around for a bit, trying to get my bearings. Then I swivel around to suddenly—contrary to any actual laws of science—come face to face with a huge, sinister-looking planet. I gasp. Immediately, I am pulled in towards this pink-purple glowing alien planet. Through it all, I flail my arms in the ether of space, trying to hold on to something—anything. But it's pointless—I'm headed towards the planet's embrace, no matter what.

There's nothing I can do in these dreams except panic. And even though many times I have known I'm in a dream, the sinking feeling in the pit of my stomach is very real. I often carry that feeling with me throughout my day, hours after I dreamt it. So it is perhaps even worse that I remember these dreams rather well. Not just the ones that recur, or are recent, but a sorry hall of fame for dreams both great and horrific. Only at twenty-seven do I begin to realize they point to an anxiety about rootlessness, a desperation for an anchoring.

Over the years, the way I've travelled has changed. Planes have almost single-handedly replaced trains and buses for travel, and it has exacted a sort of disbelief from me that runs constantly like an app in the background. Travel is too short, too unreal. Is it really possible that in the space of three hours—the length of a Hindi movie, or a delicious afternoon snooze—I'm in a whole different country? A blink, and I'm in a park in

Vancouver; another, and I'm in the Metro, gliding through the majestic Delhi cityscape in a smoggy, weakly sunlit winter. Blink. Blink. Blink. I continue to move cities with stunning nimbleness, whether I'm present in the moment or not.

I constantly tell myself I have many homes—Delhi, Pune, Bengaluru, Chennai, Hyderabad, Vancouver, Gurgaon, Mumbai—but that kind of affirmation works only on the good days. On other days, I know that's at best a delicate construction of the truth. The people I love inhabit these cities, and while I know, without a doubt, that I'll always have a place in their homes, there's no one place that houses all of me.

I have split like an amoeba—my favourite childhood books gathering dust and moss in a damp storeroom in Gurgaon even until just a few months ago, my favourite winter jacket stowed under a bed-storage space, my favourite tea cups in my friend Iman's house in blue-grey Vancouver, all important documents following the trail of wherever my parents are at the moment. On a conscious level, this doesn't affect me. I know by now that when I meet someone new in a city I've moved to, chances are I'll have a couple of years with them at most. So I come up with a system that maximizes efficiency. Get close, but make no promises of forever. Get closer, because there are no promises of forever. On the outside, I have made my peace with this life, the only kind of life I've known. But it is clear to me now that my dreams indicate otherwise. I'm constantly bracing myself for being thrown out of my loved ones' orbit.

This anxiety of rootlessness, this weightlessness, manifests in many ways. At twenty-one, I was diagnosed with polycystic ovary syndrome (PCOS), a complex metabolic disorder that affects one in four women in India. One of the symptoms and/or consequences (depending on which chicken or egg causation theory you believe) is sudden weight gain. I found myself, over the course of two months, many kilos heavier. The first doctor I went to, for PCOS, at the age of twenty-three, said I had brought the syndrome upon myself because I was staying up all night and had no routine, no self-respect.

I wasn't told about the increased cortisol (stress) and insulin levels that often come with PCOS, creating an insatiable hunger that constantly demands food in exchange for chronic fatigue. I've lived with PCOS for the past fourteen years now, and am only just coming to terms with how much it demands of me every day. The weight is easy to cling to, hard to let go of. The only options that do work often border dizzyingly on the lines of an eating disorder. On particularly indulgent days, I have wondered if it isn't another way in which my body is trying to ground itself psychologically—perhaps calculating that this excess weight will anchor me, will make sure I'm too heavy to be lifted out of orbits. That it never works is, of course, of no consequence.

There is something I best get out of the way for now. It really is tempting to draw connections between my metaphors of weight and weightlessness and my literal weight, given that

I've spent a chunk (ha!) of my twenties overweight. It wouldn't be an invalid connection to make, but it is to me, for now, an unimportant one. Once the raw shock of looking at my body in trial rooms wore away around the age of twenty-two, I stopped processing my life through my size. I just stopped looking at myself in the mirror. I'd overestimate and buy the largest size any shop had. Of course, I have, over the years, come to learn that this is more a reflection on the restrictive sizes in mainstream retail than on anything else, but I'm not sure this knowledge would have significantly improved my self-esteem at twenty. I've had countless issues with my body, but weight very quickly stopped being one of them.

But I'm getting ahead of myself here. For now, perhaps a small note on writing about an unremarkable life: There's a question that comes up quite often in hypothetical scenarios, and it is supposed to be indicative of a crucial facet of your personality. If you could have a superpower, and had to pick between invisibility or teleportation, the question goes, which would you choose? Having experienced both invisibility and teleportation, I know that my answer is neither.

And yet, grudgingly, I somehow seem to have mastered both.

This is the story of that alchemy.

Hunger

Until Varun came into our lives, when I was a little over four, it was just me and my parents. I was supposed to be a September child, but popped out in the first week of August. I seem to have made sure to time it perfectly on a Sunday morning, sometime around 10 a.m., neither too early nor too late in the day. Just two hours away from being the perfect brunch baby we were all promised.

Born to folks who are both given to varying degrees of emotional stoicism, I roughed up against their quiet expressions of love with my vulgar way of first naming my need and then openly asking for it. Almost all my childhood stories, across accounts, paint the picture of a happy, confident child who is self-satisfied and loves being the centre of attention. It seems odd that two quiet, reserved and mild-mannered people could come together to produce a child with such an appetite for love and attention.

There's a picture of my parents holding me a few weeks after I was born. My mother, slender in a pastel pink nightgown and a thick braid, which looks like it weighs more than the rest of her body, my father, in a muslin white kurta and windswept hair—both of them so very young and gawky, curved like brackets around me. Their faces are turned away from the camera, so you can only catch indications of what they might look like. In the hands of a male author, Amma would probably be described as beautiful and waifish, her deep-set round eyes forever ready to hold your gaze, something about her giving you the idea that she won't be tamed, or suchlike. Nanna would be spared these condescending personality derivations and described rather mechanically, as square-jawed and bony, a face that could only just about balance that impressive set of teeth that often broke into a full-toothed smile, ready to ease the tension in any room. Both of them are holding me gingerly—and this might as well be my projection—proud and scared.

It does me good to remember that, despite the hubris of self-narration, I'm only a second-generation, displaced, no-culture kid. Amma and Nanna grew up, much like I did—and perhaps in many ways worse—everywhere. As the eldest of three, Amma was often brought up by relatives during the times my grandparents would move across the country for my grandfather's job. When I'm aghast at this abandonment, Amma reminds me that to her father, leaving her behind was an act of love. He wanted her to have a steady childhood, a continuity of experiences she could bank on as the rest of her family (which soon included her younger sister and brother, six and eleven years apart, too young to be left behind) did the legwork. In a world where moving was a necessity, my grandfather (Tathaiyya to me) wanted to give Amma the luxury of staying put as much as he could. As a result, Amma often grew up outside of her immediate family. She stayed with uncles, aunts, cousins, whoever was around and ready to host another child into their already brimming mix. The stories my aunt and my mother tell me about growing up, thus, are given to being rather different. I don't think Amma's resentful of being left behind; or she had already made some kind of peace with it by the time she passed these stories on to her children. I wonder if she, like me, sometimes reads abandonment in the place of love.

When Amma was around eight, her family moved to what was then Calcutta. Tathaiyya had decided that Amma would stay behind in Hyderabad and continue her schooling there. Amma was to enter fourth standard, and Tathaiyya felt it would be a risk to pull her out of school then, especially when he had no idea where they would be posted in Calcutta, and what the schools would be like. Ammama, my grandmother, however, wouldn't hear of it. After a lot of emotional outbursts in Calcutta, Tathaiyya found himself on a train to Hyderabad to pick up his firstborn and spend, perhaps for the first time in their cumulative lives, some time alone with each other.

Amma tells me that Tathaiyya could be quite fond of people, but had a hard time expressing it. Their father-daughter relationship was marked by both the distinct texture of awkwardness with a firstborn and the emotional ecosystem of their times. Amma was intimidated by him, and perhaps he as much, by a child he loved but didn't really know. Unsurprising, then, that the joy Amma felt at having her father turn up to take her home very quickly changed to shyness. As much as she loved her father, he was to her, until then, always at arm's length. The journey back to Calcutta, thus, was spent in awkward silence. When they got off at the train station in Calcutta, Amma was overwhelmed by how crowded it was. Tathaiyya wasn't used to supervising children and walked briskly ahead of Amma, unmindful of how crowds ebb and flow to eat up people and belongings you don't keep close enough. Scared of losing him, but even more scared of expressing this fear, Amma lightly held on to the end of Tathaiyya's shirt as they snaked their way through the crowd. 'I was petrified of losing sight of him, but I didn't want him to know I was there,' she tells me.

This is a refrain that comes up often when Amma talks about her childhood, this not wanting to be found. Perhaps out of an innateness, or perhaps in reaction to her early years, or maybe both, Amma only asked of life to remain indistinguishable in the background. You see, for an eight-year-old who didn't know how to read and write proficiently in any one language (because she moved across schools in different states, each with its own local language), attention usually meant embarrassment and humiliation. In Calcutta, she soon found out that where her sister spoke Bengali fluently already, she couldn't communicate at all. All she knew was Telugu, our mother tongue, a language pretty much useless in a Catholic school in West Bengal. Amma was smart, so it's not like she didn't understand, but because she didn't stay long enough in any one city, all her knowledge was intuitive, something she understood but couldn't produce. My mother—knower of four languages by then, speaker of none.

As she grew up like this, two things happened (which passed on to her children as well)—she picked up a flair for languages and found constancy in books. By the time she entered her teenage years, Amma already knew she wanted to pass through life without anyone noticing she was there. A small steady job, perhaps, with the possibility of books, a non-threatening life that looped into herself. At sixteen, she discovered William Somerset Maugham in her college library. In one of his books, Maugham writes something about wanting to move through life without attracting the attention of fate, and Amma fell in literary love. Through her growing-up years, Amma pored through books, magazines, newspapers, railway timetables, discarded flyers—anything she could get her hands on, not wanting to be found. 'Oh, Padma!' she'd often hear. 'You're here as well! I didn't notice you.' As tempting as it is for me to read abject pathos into her childhood, I remind myself that this is what Amma wanted—it is what made her happy. Where I would read melancholia into her life, she read happiness. And lest anyone be misled into imagining someone quiet, demure and easy to push over, I must press upon the person that she is quick-witted and resilient, an incredible mimic with a sharp tongue that can cut you to pieces with a straight face—in at least five languages.

Where self-articulation is always ready at the tip of Amma's tongue, Nanna asks me for time to collect his thoughts. I wonder if this is because Amma has sat with her thoughts often. It's only fair that I ask them for their stories, inviting them for this self-fashioning, this crafting of their personalities, since I get to do it across the expanse of this book. So I let Nanna take his time, and regularly check in to see if he has anything for me. It's not that he doesn't remember, but simply thinks it is nothing worth writing about.

As the third of five children, and as one amongst many cousins living in the same house, Nanna's role in the family necessitated that he make himself useful in the mass of extended family living on meagre means. Like Amma, he and his family moved around in his childhood, although not as frequently. Unlike Amma, who was separated from family and also from her siblings because of their age gap, Nanna grew up with his brothers and sister in tow, closer to each other in age, a hive mind of sorts. In a wave of people living together like that, Nanna says, no one really had the luxury to pay you any particular attention. And although Tatha (Nanna's father) was a lot more expressive than Tathaiyya with both his love and his disdain, Nanna and his siblings' relationship with him was marked by the characteristic of their times—stilted and awkward, but filled with intimidation and love. As a result of growing up in a household like theirs, marred by a lack of money and the iron fist of patriarchy, Nanna and his younger brother grew up being especially close to their mother, my Maamma.

Where Amma was often alone in this abandonment, Nanna always had his siblings. When he was around five, Tatha had to work out of town for a while, in Bangalore (as it was known even till a few years back). As soon as the train from Parvathipuram, Andhra Pradesh, reached Bangalore, the kids jumped on to the platform and, once they spotted Tatha, ran towards him. As Tatha hugged each of his children, Nanna waited his turn in the background. 'And who is this fellow?' Tatha asked out loud. It took a second for everyone to realize that it was not an endearment—my grandfather really didn't know which of the kids he was. Nanna insists that though this is a memory that has resisted erosion and the erasure of the years, it is not something that has traumatized him. 'It's natural when there are twenty of you in the family, with all the young boys around the same age, always together. Nannagaaru worked most of the time, and didn't spend too much time with us whenever he was home. So it's not like he was putting in any effort to not remember me. It's just something we've chuckled about over the years,' Nanna says.

Right after Nanna passed fifth standard in Srikakulam,

Tatha got posted to Chennai. He wanted his children to study in a school that taught under the central board, especially since they were given to moving so much. Nanna and his siblings would thus have to learn Hindi as their second language. Nanna and his sister, Rajani, had to appear for an entrance exam to be eligible for school admission, writing an English-medium examination to enter the sixth and eighth standards, respectively. They both sat on their seats, amiable and smiling, poised for excellence. Except for the little fact that they didn't know a word of English outside of the alphabet. Back home, in Srikakulam, the children would have learnt English only in eighth standard, so apart from the little smattering of English they heard at home when Tatha worked, Nanna and Rajani Attha (paternal aunt) were at a complete loss. Nanna still remembers the invigilator in the room that day, a teacher named Girija, who would keep walking by him and Attha. Noticing that neither of them was writing a word, she asked them something. In English. The two just smiled and nodded amiably in return. They were thrown out of the classroom, and refused admission.

When Tatha heard about this, he stormed to the school with Nanna and Attha in tow, and cornered the principal outside her office. 'They're only children,' he pleaded. 'This is what they're supposed to do. Given them a chance, they will learn.' Partly perhaps moved by Tatha's argument and partly because it would be easier to give them admission than not, the principal agreed. But because of where they stood with their English proficiency in an English-medium school, they had to backtrack two whole years. Nanna entered fourth standard, and Attha sixth.

Nanna entered a class that spoke mostly in Tamil with each other, and in English with the teachers. New, unable to communicate with anyone and with a remarkable crop of spiky, untameable hair that refused to behave, he entered a situation ripe for teasing and bullying. But Nanna was also a good two years older than everyone else in the classroom, and as they soon found out, a natural at sports. It wasn't long before he slipped into this new school, this new life. 'Even if things didn't revolve around me,' he says, 'you could say I was at the centre of things in class.' He and Attha soon picked up Tamil, as one would perhaps do when one was young and thrown into the deep end of an alien language, immersed in it, day in and day out. With English, though, Nanna put in a little more effort. 'Tatha seemed to have a mild disdain for people who couldn't speak English. I'm not sure if that disdain was correct, or something that I'd share now, but back then, I wanted his validation,' Nanna tells me.

Where Amma's character-building happened solitarily, in a corner where she fought hard to keep to herself and away from others, Nanna's happened in the thick of things, at the centre of the party. If you ask him, though, he will maintain that the character-building started only when Amma came into his life when he was twenty.

The story of how they met and why they fell in love is perhaps not mine to tell, or at least not in this book. I joke even now that my parents must each have secretly had a penchant for the dramatic, and because they had to stifle it, their combined unfulfilled desires formed me. I was born, I say to them, to balance out what they each were forced to put aside. If one were to paint an exaggerated comparison between my parents' childhood and mine, where they plodded through their lives determined to renounce it, I was born with a pit in my stomach, hungry for everything.

But that would at best be only a half-truth. I was certainly predisposed to the dramatic, but also built a muscle for it in reaction to a situation out of my control at the age of two, when Amma had a miscarriage. The baby had almost come to full term but died of asphyxiation when the umbilical cord wrapped around its neck, slowly strangling it. The doctors caught this very late into the pregnancy, so Amma had to deliver a stillborn.

I remember snatches from that time, mostly visuals without audio, a grainy silent movie. My father carrying me on his hip, us standing near Amma's hospital bed, my grandmother coaxing her to eat something, Amma's head weakly indicating no. The miscarriage was also threatening Amma's life, and the journey back from that loss and hospitalization was traumatic for everyone involved. Up until then, Amma tells me, I was an independent kid. As soon as I was capable, I started brushing my teeth on my own, picking out my clothes, dressing and feeding myself. During the course of the hospitalization, however, I seem to have regressed and claimed to not know how to do anything. I needed my father to do all of this for me. Amma, of course, is a lot kinder to me when she remembers this. 'It must have shaken your world, to not understand what was going on. A child can't help but pick up the energy in the room. Everyone around you was worried and stressed, and I had suddenly disappeared from your life.'

How much of our personalities are innate, and how much is hastily slapped together in the wake of childhood crises? Did my primal feeling of Amma always being slightly out of reach, unwilling to hold me and love me, stem from that incident? It would seem so, given that the person I loved the most was inexplicably out of sight, and when in sight, painfully out of my reach. How many days had I watched Amma grow weaker and weaker, propped up in my father's steady but exhausted arms? I had no way to understand my mother's pregnancy, my parents' tragic loss, and the looming threat of another. Only my own loss. With Amma in the hospital, I had been placed under many kind neighbours' care until Nanna could come back to take care of me. All I knew was that my mother didn't live with us any more and that she wouldn't hold me.

In a lot of new-age philosophy, the stomach is supposed to be where you hold your vision of the world. People with weak stomachs cannot digest the world *as it is* because they always dream of an ideal, moralistic other. I'm not sure what it adds to my reading of hunger and appetite and processing, except that as far back as Amma or I can remember, I've had a weak stomach. I was born with colic, and continued to have gastrointestinal flare-ups throughout my childhood. If there is any truth to this philosophy, could it be just that? All that discomfort and pain—just an incapability to process the world as it really is? Could I really not just move on with life, knowing I was loved in the deepest way my parents could love me? On the other hand, what was it about my need for attention that both amused my parents and made them so uncomfortable?

Decades later, I stumbled upon this bit from one of my favourite poets, Alice Oswald, in a poem titled *The Fox*. I offer it up as a shorthand cheat code to this entire section, a codex that contains every element of the threads I wanted to gently pull together from my life. I can take my entire life and weigh it against these four lines, and watch how they decipher the inexpressible:

Just so abrupt and odd/
the way she went/
hungrily asking/
in the heart's thick accent

Nanna's side of the family is gregarious, made up of folks easy and expressive with their emotions. There's some musical talent that runs through the generations, but an even larger flair for performance, sometimes disproportionate to actual skill. There are two things that happen when my father's side gets together. There's a lot of singing, and a lot of scatalogical humour.

How many Buddhavarapus does it take to screw on a light bulb? How many ever are not in a bathroom taking proud, gigantic shits.

Individually, they tend to be majestically temperamental folks, but when they come together—this clattering, stumbling wave of a family, especially in times of death and mourning—they're a hive mind of comfort and laughter. There are tears, of course, but there's always laughter. When Maamma passed away in 2011, my uncles and aunt came together to perform her last rites in our house in Delhi. There was so much laughter ringing out from our open front door that the neighbours found it all a bit distasteful in an atmosphere that demanded gravitas and mourning.

Nanna's family was a little less well off than my mother's when they were growing up. It was, in Nanna's early years, a hand-to-mouth existence, with the children hoarding their food sometimes, unsure of when their next meal would be. It wasn't like that always, he reminds me, but they certainly knew what it was like to go to bed hungry—something

Varun and I don't. It's because it was a joint family, mostly of unemployed young men at the time, a victim of their own ill-fitting education and the times. And in a family where the contours swung wildly to accommodate as many relatives as possible, averaging around twenty, for a while it was only Tatha who was bringing in any money.

Amma's side of the family was marginally better, helped in part by the fact that everyone lived in nuclear families. They're extremely private, tending towards emotional reticence, and impressively thrifty. I remain unconvinced that there is no connection between the two. Where Nanna's family is made up of hearty, unafraid spenders who value the feeling of a good (spontaneous) buy over the permanence of money, my mother's side is more judicious. There is no such thing as an indulgence that you haven't saved up for. Though they rarely had any money to spare, my mother says they never went hungry.

Little surprise, then, that Varun and I have an ingrained sense of respect for food. Hours spent agonizing over wasted food on plates were scribbled guiltily inside diaries, whispered as confessions to parents. So I ended up eating—and this is typical—everything on my plate. It is usually mistaken for gluttony, but it really is an unconscious anxiety of leaving food on my plate.

Having grown up in a family that believes in cooking more portions than necessary at any given time, especially when guests come over (there should always be enough food), it always makes us a little awkward to eat at a house where the portions appear small. The serving bowls are tiny, so each of us quickly, mentally calculates and approximates how little to serve ourselves so that no one is stuck with the horror and ignominy of having finished the food. Unsure, I suppose, of whether this is all there is, or there is more of each back in the kitchen. The calculations are nerve-racking. What is supposed to be a comforting meal becomes, instead, one of calculations to avoid any embarrassing moment. What if one of us asks if there is more dal? What if we're eating this sparingly, but there is a lot more food inside and we're only making our hosts distraught at how little we're eating?

Back at home, you see, it's the visual of larger portions that we use, as symbol, as sign, as signifier, to convey this: *Do not approximate, this is feeling, not mathematics, eat till your heart bursts.* As the years go by, I realize how much of all this is a privilege—to be able to cook more, have more and, even if it takes other sacrifices, to have the immense luxury to prioritize food over everything else.

Another habit I notice is how my father and I clean up and organize table clutter post meals, especially when eating outside our house. We polish off our plates, stack the spoons and plates and cups together, go around the table collecting wares, organizing them in neat piles that can then be picked up easily. My mother and brother, on the other hand, draw distinct territories between their food items. Nothing touches the other.

Look at all of us, I often think to myself, so reassured in our belief that we can afford the sacrifices of impermanence, but our fingers on a dinner table bely this, each pair involved in a silent symphony, itching for things to stack up, for order.

Unlike a lot of babies whose primary taste of food, outside of breast or formula milk, is sweet, I was weaned on the savoury. As much as it was my parents' choice to just feed me rice or dal blitzed in the blender, I'm told it was mine too. Once I reached a particular milestone, my mother bought Cerelac, a popular baby-food formula. I must have been somewhere between one and two years old, and was supposed to have one-third of the packet for a meal. Apparently, I kept asking for more, until I finished the box in one sitting. That's when my parents decided I was better off just eating what the adults were, blended in a mixie.

I also ate erratically through my childhood. I'd eat my heart's fill for a day, and then not feel hungry for another two—nibbling my way around whatever was offered to me. When my mother checked with the doctor, she was assured that these were teething issues, that as long as I was feeling hungry and eating at some point, it would temper itself out.

Reader, it never did.

What little discipline I've had towards food has been nurtured painstakingly.

Whenever I had worms in my stomach as a child, I'd find myself waking up my father at night. I used to wake my mother up—I always sought her attention first—but she slept heavier than my father and didn't have much to offer me except a cuddle, and patted me till I slept, next to her, but worming around in discomfort. My father, I realized, was not only incredibly easy to wake up, but he would also make the itching go away. He'd make me sit in his spot on the bed, still warm from his leaving, go to the kitchen and make a drink of sugar water for me. I'd drink the mixture and, almost immediately, the itching would stop. Here was an undeniable hero who loved me until I had my fill, and also made the worms go away.

Years later, when I accuse my mother, only half-jokingly, of abandoning me on my midnight wormy adventures, she scoffs. 'Please, Shruti. I was better than your father,' she says, 'who was bribing the worms with sugar water so they'd calm down and let him sleep.' I look at my father, who laughs sheepishly. What a traitor.

'In fact,' she reminds me, 'who was it that would give you deworming medicine the next morning?' I reel under this exposé. All this while I had mistaken my mother's soothing *me* to sleep as refusal to care, and found love in my father's act of soothing juicy, fat intestinal worms to sleep instead.

I keep coming back to this incident because there's something so essential about my relationships with each of them to glean from here. A do-it-yourself metaphor for any situation in life involving my parents—my mother attempting to cure things quietly through restraint and necessary withholding, and my father through exaggerated gestures he knows we'll all be too embarrassed to say we want. And, rather typically, because my father so freely and physically expressed his love, I sought validation from my mother. I was not worthy until I had impressed her, won her love, earned her love.

Love, attention, stories, food, knowledge—I was hungry for it all. Which is why when, at twenty-one, I found myself scrummaging through food deep into the night, it didn't strike me as anything out of the fleetingly ordinary. At some point, I suppose, all that I was consuming and rejecting, both emotionally and literally, had to start showing.

Story

When I was around six or seven, my mother gifted me a book of fairy tales during my summer holidays. I hurriedly opened it to find inside an inscription that would stay with me forever:

Dear Shruti,
Happy days are here again!

It was a beautiful indigo hardcover and I inhaled every story that summer, running my hands over the inscription neatly filled out in my mother's unmistakable cursive. To date, the language to tailor the feelings that the inscription evoked in me doesn't exist. Amma, especially during my formative years, was guarded with her articulation of love. Unlike with Nanna, who was at once verbose and affectionate, I felt like I was at least an arm's length away from her at all times. In that rootlessness of being six, having a new young brother, moving once again to a new city, my mother had gifted me a dazzling indigo hardcover for no reason at all. I was so thrilled that it was addressed to me. That my mother took the time to pick something out and write something in it *only for me*.

Happy days are here again!

Swayed by the gospel of her words, I registered for the first time an ecstasy. Yes, yes, indeed we were happy! These *were* happy days—school was out and my mother loved me. But something else happened in that reading too, something I didn't realize until decades later. Happy days were here, *again*. Did that mean they had left? That we hadn't inhabited happy days for a while? Had we just passed by days (*who knew how long? Days? Months? Years? When were you happy last, Amma?*) bereft of happiness? Nestled within that delirium of happy days being there was the slowly unravelling, paralysing fear that they had also been taken away, and that I had been completely blind to it.

Here I was, at six, my one aching desire to write fluently in cursive and own a Milton water bottle transformed by a blue book into a rhetorician.

Unfortunately for everyone around me, I started talking when I was only eight months old. Much to my parents' alternating pride and chagrin, I seemed to have skipped the baby-talk phase. I say 'I' skipped it as if it were an indicator of my genius, but truth is that I skipped baby talk because my parents skipped baby talk. I spoke quickly, and a lot—ready to put forth at the slightest. Legend goes that no matter what time of day or night it was, I'd appear at the slightest movement, the lightest murmur, the quaking of a leaf, the sound of a leaky tap, a stifled sneeze, ready to pick up exactly where I had left off in my droning PowerPoint presentation.

Of these early years, my mother told me two stories, between which I think you can triangulate an essential part of my personality, a piece to the puzzle that you never signed up to solve. The first is about a pair of shoes and the toilet.

I was around one or two years old, and we were living in Delhi, when my parents had some friends over. A great time was had by all, until one of the guests discovered, right before they were about to leave, that their shoes were missing. Cue frantic search for said shoes. How could a pair of shoes disappear from *inside* the house? My mother then saw me, strolling by rather casually, and got that kind of inexplicable feeling a parent gets when they know their child has been up to no good. She then proceeded to ask me if I knew where the guest's shoes were, taking her chance with a nonplussed one-year-old. I nodded and told her they were in the toilet. Aghast, everyone made their way to the bathroom, to indeed find the guest's shoes wedged inside the toilet bowl—and water everywhere. I had not just shoved them there, I had tried violently to flush them down. 'Why didn't you tell us? We were searching for them all this while!' my mother asked, baffled. On this matter, Tiny Shruti only shrugged and said, 'You never asked.'

A few months later, my parents and I were about to head out the door when Amma found her house keys missing from her bag. This time around, she didn't waste time searching. Did I have anything to do with the keys, she asked me immediately. 'Yes, I threw them out of the window,' I confirmed gravely, and sat myself down for what was going to be a long treasure hunt. Nanna was sent outside the house to search for them, while my mother directed him from inside, routinely checking in with me about the general ambit and direction of the said projectile throw. Despite Nanna's most valiant efforts in the ditch outside our house, there were no keys to be found. As the three of us sat in the living room (two of us really defeated), my mother unconsciously rummaged through her purse and found the keys there. Amma was puzzled. Why would I lie? On this topic, Tiny Shruti only confirmed, 'I wanted to.'

Although I am the veritable protagonist of both these incidents, they are from so far back in my timeline that I have no organic memory of them. I received these stories as if they were of a third person, which they might as well have been (*do you remember how it was to be you in the past?*). This experiential difference—me not remembering the incidents—allows me to read them with, I'd like to think, a certain detachment. Even without an articulation for it, I had tapped into something crucial about words—they were heady, electric, and gave you a strange power if you used them right.

By the time my family and I had moved from Delhi to Bengaluru to Mumbai, I had escalated to telling really elaborate, outlandish stories to anyone who'd buy them. The only life I knew with any authority was my own, so those were the stories I told. If it so happened that I ran in short stock, I made some up. From a herd of students 'trampling' upon me during a stampede on a staircase in a new school, to my teacher hanging me off the classroom door for not doing my homework, my imagined life was filled with strife, which I would, of course, always valiantly and with exceptional acumen survive. By the time we moved from Mumbai to Ahmedabad, I was a seven-year-old bona fide peddler of stories. Like builders who knocked on wooden walls to identify which part was hollow, I'd knock around, testing the crowd, before I could find a hollow.

One of my favourites is where I got bored at school and pretended it was my birthday. I casually dropped it during a conversation with a friend in class. She shared her lunch with me that day as a gift. A few weeks later, when it was actually my birthday and I was sent from home wearing a casual dress, she caught my lie. Without a moment's hesitation, I explained her confusion away: It was rather simple, you see, I was born twice. I had initially come out of my mother's womb in July, except that my nose hadn't been formed yet. So, like a cake in the oven that was just mildly undone, I was shoved back into my poor mother's toasty oven-womb until my nose formed, and then came out perfect in August.

But let me not deceive you into believing I only peddled stories, like a neighbourhood toddler drug lord. I was constantly breaking the cardinal rule of dealing: 'Don't get high off your own supply.' I consumed stories at nearly double the rate I doled them out. A kindergarten teacher once threatened to let 'the ogre' who lived in the storeroom of our classroom out because we were being so noisy. Every other five-year-old comprehended perfectly that this was a ruse—all tell, no show. But I was petrified and started crying. Exasperated, and in a 'you cannot be serious' tone, my friend turned towards me and told me not to cry because it was all a lie—there was no ogre, surely I knew they didn't exist? 'Yes, yes,' I nodded through tearful hiccups, embarrassed that everyone but I seemed to know this. 'I'm crying because my stomach's hurting.'

Although the stories were made up, painfully awkward for any listener, I can't help but read into them. I suppose if one were to be particularly kind, you could say these stories were my security blanket against the trauma of moving, of always being the new girl in any classroom. Why couldn't I just tell my parents the truth? That I had got humiliated by a teacher on my first day for not knowing something the class had already learnt, and that kids around me—who I was hoping would want to come talk to me during the break—had sniggered. That some girl lightly shoved me as we made a beeline for PT. Or that someone in another classroom, in another city, on another of my first days as new girl, looked at the thick dosas condensing in my lunch box and exclaimed, 'Ewwwww! What is that?'

Why couldn't I just tell my parents that first days were hard, and that a new life was harder, that making friends was a tense, frightening process? Why couldn't I find the words to tell my father how I felt when I let go of his hand just before I entered a classroom; the trepidation I felt, through my fingers, as his footsteps slowed down and came to a stop before the door. The slight shake in my legs as I gingerly entered the room, gathering courage to look everyone in the eye and just hoping that one of them, any of them, would look back at me and smile. Perhaps there was no language for these feelings back then. And so it seemed important to Tiny Shruti that she relay these stories, in exactly as much intensity and outrageousness as she imagined them, because I sense (now) that it was exactly how she felt them.

I was imagining a parallel life in which I was the centre of everything, of course, but also a world in which words would actually do justice to feelings, and once articulated, would immediately be acted upon. I figured out soon enough that saying I had a stomach ache would allow me to stay at home, but saying I was too scared wouldn't. Pretending my fingers hurt was less embarrassing to explain than to tell Nanna that I didn't want him to go to work and that I missed him while he was gone. And so I'd lie, often and flamboyantly. I'd keep transferring and projecting all my emotions on to physical manifestations because it felt like I could finally translate one pain into another that the world would understand—or, at least, take seriously.

To be sure, I didn't read any of these experiences as traumatic then. They just were what they were. I had a childhood mostly filled with laughter, happiness and lots of love. It is now, on recall, that the meaning of these experiences change. As I trace my anxieties in this present moment, it shouldn't be surprising to me that they lead back to the very beginning.

In English Literature 101, we're taught how to recognize 'unreliable narrators' in a text. It's a tool used in both fiction and non-fiction, where the person narrating the tale is not to be depended upon. They might even make a show of how frank and honest they are, how they confide everything in you, the reader. But for whatever it is worth, they turn out to have either hidden some things from you, or intentionally misled you into thinking one way when it was another. To me, there was nothing duplicitous about these narrators. We're all unreliable narrators, because narration is unreliable. They shift and squirm and thrum under your fingers, mould meaning into a thousand ways, waiting to be whatever it is the listener is open to receiving. There is a truth in unreliability.

Around the age of twelve or thirteen, though, just when I was about to make a big move from Mumbai to Delhi, the elaborate, impeccably and intricately crafted stories abruptly disappeared.

Love

I'd like to think that I understood, even at an age where I could not articulate it, that love was somehow different from attention. I don't think I ever doubted that I was loved, and didn't particularly only want attention from my parents. I think it was this understanding that made me easy-going. My parents could go to restaurants and leave me with the staff and enjoy their meal, while I lapped up the special attention. It is perhaps the only thing I knew about love—that it was given to you. It wasn't until I turned four, until Varun came into our lives, that I understood that I was also capable of giving love and attention.

Surer than they were about having a biological child, my parents knew they wanted to adopt. The plan, if life were to ever allow it, was to adopt a child and perhaps have a biological one. But there was me, and after me that painful miscarriage. Even when they thought they were going to have two biological children, my parents decided they would adopt a third. A year or two after Amma's hospitalization, when I was first told about the possibility of an adopted sibling, I apparently claimed that if this process meant that my mother wouldn't have to go to a hospital again, I was all for it. There's so much I've forgotten since, but how I met Varun is seared into my memory.

We're in an auto, turning a corner into a quiet lane with lots of trees. On the left side of the street is the orphanage, which looks like a cottage to me. I skip and jump using Nanna's wrist for leverage as we make our way inside to meet a nun. Amma and Nanna sit on chairs while I stand between them, trying to hoist myself up using the arms of the chairs. The nun is talking to Amma and Nanna. None of this is of interest to me. I continue trying to hoist myself up. Then, someone brings a baby out, and I suddenly find myself staring at a five-month-old in a small orange cardigan that barely covers his chest. I peer over my father's shoulder and look closely at this semi-naked child. I loom over his face and laugh, because he is naked and naked means shame and naked means funny. The baby looks up at me, unsure for a couple of seconds. He mimics my gesture, and gurgles, and puts his tiny hand on my cheek. I smart at the touch. In all the ways I have been loved by my parents so far in my four years, I have never felt what I feel in this moment.

Little Varun Rao looked at me that day with his big dinner-plate eyes and I found, for perhaps the first time, a love that was rooted outside of myself. I discovered the capacity to register love, finally, as a verb.

I prepared for months before Varun was to come home. I practised holding an imaginary baby in front of the television, mollifying it by pointing at it, believing it would be overwhelmed by the logic of my offering and immediately stop crying. Yes, I would be the baby whisperer of this house, I decided. It was all taken care of, and I continued my homework until the day he came home.

But then Varun came home and no one let me hold him on my own. Worse, I had zero sway over his moods, and no amount of signalling at the television would make him stop crying. The only way I could hold him was if I sat next to an adult, padded on all sides by pillows. Naturally, I grew bored of being a brand-new sister very quickly. It had no perks and the baby couldn't even talk. The only positive aspect in my life that the baby brought was some kind of street-cred in my apartment complex. My bully would run to his mother and demand a baby sister immediately. I wasn't without sibling jealousy, though. When everyone was crowded around the months-old Varun as he tried to turn over to his side, ooh-ing, aah-ing, cheering him on, I rolled up next to Varun and turned myself over. 'Come on, folks!' I wanted to say, 'I can do it!' Like a dog performing a trick no one asked it to.

While growing up, Varun and I were very attached. He adored me and believed everything I said. The first joke I ever created out of thin air became his first joke. It was curious in that it had absolutely no punchline, but for some reason it made Varun laugh a lot. And he'd tell it to everyone proudly. 'Mickey Mouse went into a forest (very important to use references that the child understands) and he saw some poop. And then he ate it.' Varun laughed for days. I had found my audience at last—and dear god did I milk it!

Varun was typically non-committal about everything—nothing fazed him, nothing seemed to hurt or anger or affect him. But because he had pledged allegiance to me, my battles became our battles and he'd give me company out of his generosity and love for me, boosting both numbers and morale. When we first moved into a house in Mumbai, Amma and Nanna's room had an air-conditioning unit attached to it. I remember one summer, when they switched on the AC, I was so angry that they would turn it on for themselves and expect me and my brother to sleep in our own room. I stomped back to our room and told Varun, 'They're switching on the AC, and they said we can't join them! How mean.' Varun shrugged as if to say, 'Oh? Okay', and that was to be the end of that. Except, of course, it wasn't. I pacified my already pacifist brother, saying, 'Okay, no need to worry. They can have their dumb AC—it stinks of pigeon poop anyway. But we have the power of imagination, okay? When we go to sleep, you have to imagine we're in a mountain full of snow and it's coooooollllldddddd, yes?' Poor Varun agreed, and we both slept thinking of cold things like snow and cold people like our parents.

The next morning, when Amma came to wake us both up for school, she noticed Varun's body was hot to the touch. He was running a high fever. 'How did you get yourself a fever overnight...' Amma mumbled, as she took the thermometer out of his mouth. 'It's because of Shukka,' Varun insisted. (In Telugu, 'akka' means elder sister, and 'Shruti Akka' was too much for Varun to say, so I became Shukka, first to him, then to everyone in my extended family.) 'She told me to imagine how it would feel to sleep on snow...she told me,' my too-pure-for-this-world brother said. In his head, he had imagined so seriously, so intensely, that being out in the snow gave him a fever. And they say that creative people don't make a physical impact.

Despite the four-year gap between Varun and I, we grew up as one unit. I'd talk to him about my life and its various dramatics as if he were also eight, and not a snotty four-year-old. In turn, my parents would also treat us as a package deal. They wouldn't scold one of us without scolding the other. I suppose it came from the noble ideal of fairness, so whenever one of them was in the mood to lecture, it was a free-for-all. If you as much as heard a whisper of a lecture in another room, you avoided passing by at all cost. I was (and remain) quite fearful of authority at the end of the day, so, despite my cunning wiles, I was well behaved. This meant that Varun ended up doing more (fun) things that needed lecturing, but it wasn't uncommon for me to unwittingly stroll by my parents lecturing him in one room and immediately hear Nanna call out to me, 'You! Where do you think *you're* going?'

As minimally mischievous as kids could be, and as minimally authoritative that parents thus had to be, such confrontations were few and far between. Nanna had a brief flirtation with projecting himself as a stern disciplinarian, but his efforts were half-baked while our resistance was warm apple pie. Lord knows where it materialized from, but Nanna had found a thin, reed-like piece of cane somewhere and thought it appropriate to hang it above the entrance to the kitchen, supposedly to strike fear in our hearts. He used it only once, and characteristically, on both of us, one after the other. Varun, for doing something, and me, for telling on him. I don't think Varun and I were traumatized from that as much as we were exasperated—the man simply was not meant to be a disciplinarian, and someone needed to stop this embarrassment. So one day, when no one was home, Varun and I used a stool and plucked the cane off its nail. We ran to the balcony with it and, violently and ceremonially, threw it out. The dictator had fallen. Democracy was here again.

On his part, and almost as if to prove our point about his ineffectiveness at being a scary figure, Nanna either didn't notice that the cane had gone missing, or even if he did, was too lazy to replace it.

If there's anything Varun and I learnt from that pithy phase in Nanna's life, though, it was the power of spectacle. Over the years, we formed a rule when it came to house pests. Varun and I would find a dead cockroach, or kill one, and lay it in the middle of our house, 'the town square', right under our dining table, to make an example out of it and warn the other cockroaches to stay away. Amma drew the line at dead rats and threatened to do the same with us if we ever tried. If they lasted for more than a week, despite all attempts to drive them away or kill them, they would earn our last name—and become a member of the Buddhavarapu family.

Tragically, but perhaps as is the course of natural order, by the time we were older, I lost my charm and authority over Varun. On a train from Mumbai to Ahmedabad in 2014, Varun and I sat next to each other, companions in a journey for six hours. He had forgotten to bring his portable gaming console with him, so he was stuck with having to make actual conversation with me. By this time, we had drifted apart a bit, separated by distance and our years, so the memory of this train journey has stayed with both of us.

The clouds followed us from Mumbai, the dark grey trail first making its presence felt as we shuttled towards the outskirts, then mutating into an almost-black threat over the shamrock green fields that bordered the states of Gujarat and Maharashtra. These were the things one noticed in fleeting glances: a vermilion umbrella moving against the neon green; cranes lazing around cows in what seemed to be paddy fields; a man in loose saffron clothes standing at the open door of a tin-roofed house built on the side of the railway track. I assumed the lady of the house had stepped inside to gather leftovers from a previous meal to give him. As the train hit its stride, galloping across state lines, Varun and I watched the streaks of fierce green zip by. 'What I really want are endless fields of weed,' he said, looking out of the window. I told him quite seriously that the trees we were looking at were, in fact, 'weed trees', and that at this time of the year, the farmers were waiting for the overripe weed fruit to fall to the ground so they could dry them in the sun and make weed.

Varun looked at me for a second with his lips both pursed and pouting (his signal for 'Really?'), and then guffawed, rounding it off with a fond shake of the head. I suddenly and dearly missed the days when he would have believed that story, googly-eyed in his devotion for whatever came out of his sister's mouth. But I suppose, as we learnt from Nanna, it is the nature of authority to end.

Life was, of course, never bereft of the other, more exciting kind of love. I always had a designated class crush from a very young age. Between all the changing of schools, it had mutated into more of a technicality than the heart's calling. I'd quickly do a recce of the class crop, make some calculations and decide who it was that would be my true love. I would keep it to myself for the rest of the school year and hardly ever think of it again, but if, at any point in time, you had asked me if I had a crush, I would have definitely answered in the affirmative. I didn't know what to do with one, but just that it seemed important to single someone out to be deserving of this special status. The heteronormative conditioning was strong, and life went on like that for a bit, untroubled and simple, until this crushing business became interactive and boys started having crushes back.

A few choice excerpts from a PG love life.

Kanishq in first standard, who had light green eyes and golden-brown hair and brought the best lunch in school. I would go over to his desk during recess and try scoring his food in exchange for mine. I thought we had a good scene going until, at a birthday party in another classmate's house, Kanishq's grandmother came to pick him up and told me I should stick to eating my own food because her grandson was going hungry. I was surprised because he had never told me he didn't want to share, and here, my first lesson, readers:

We are fulfilled only by the love we have been fed.

There was Neil in sixth standard, who I really appreciated because, amongst other things, he was just as short as I was. And in a class full of growth spurts, Neil and I seemed to have been left behind on this journey to the brave new world. 'How's the weather there?', 'What are oxygen levels like there?', we'd say to our friends, who'd come back after every vacation even taller. I was never in love with him, because he seemed to come across as a little bit too presenting of the Napolean syndrome but we got along really well otherwise. Kritika, who became the class mean girl solely by virtue of having her period first and knowing what it was like, fell in love with Neil. She declared it to everyone in class, and on a camping trip, to him. I'm unsure of whether what Neil said next was the truth, or a deflection tactic, but he blurted out that he couldn't be with her because his heart belonged to me. Ugh. I got a call from her on our landline soon after, and was asked to truthfully let her know if I wanted Neil or if she could 'have him'. I sputtered something non-committal in response, declaring I had nothing to do with boys, not when I was eleven anyway. And so life went on; everyone ignored the happenings of that hormone-laden week in the summer. Last heard (because I moved to Delhi soon after), during our school Holi celebrations, Neil threw some red colour, which happened to land on her head, and she declared they were married.

Love, I learnt, was really dramatic.

Then there was Roshan, who I briefly dated for four days when I was twelve, one of which happened to be Valentine's Day. He sent me a gift through a common friend, because which self-respecting twelve-year-old couple would actually talk to each other face to face? It was a plastic pink-and-white anklet made up of tiny beads, which I thought was sweet, despite the fact that I didn't wear jewellery. We ignored each other in class the whole day, as was norm, and I called him up on his landline to thank him in the evening. 'Dude, that's not for your foot, it's a necklace,' he told me, a little miffed. 'I'm pretty sure it's an anklet, because it's not made to fit a human neck, AND, the cover says it's an anklet,' I insisted.

'Uhh, it fit my neck, dude, what are you saying? But wear it wherever it fits you, I guess,' he replied, already over this topic. It was clear we couldn't last long, we came from two extreme schools of jewellery thought. We stayed in the same section until the year ended, and even though we stayed friends, I couldn't get the image of an anklet around Roshan's twiggy neck out of my mind.

Despite the clear lettering, I realized, love could be really, really daft.

Not long after I moved to Delhi from Mumbai, my best friend, Shalini, and I had crushes on two boys in our class. I don't even know why we bothered having them, considering we wanted nothing to do with those boys, except maybe use their names to dramatically sigh whenever a love song came on the radio. We came up with secret code names (obviously) to talk about them in class. I crushed heavily on 'Mr White' (named after a detergent) and Shalini pined for 'Bamboo Stick'(named unfortunately because he was so thin).

Such fictional love with non-fictional people lasted us a good year or two.

In tenth standard, I told another best friend, Girish, that I was in love with him and he sent me back a note during class, in which he drew a progress bar that said, 'I also like you 75%.' The seniors in my school van wouldn't stop bellowing like buffaloes when I showed them the note, and the laughter rang all the 23 kilometres of the bumpy, dusty road that separated school and home.

Love was uncommunicative, dramatic, daft, fictional and, sometimes, a progress bar.

The longest serious relationship in my life lasted somewhere between the ages of nineteen and twenty-three. My approximation of the time we spent together, I'm sure, rather embarrassingly indicates that the borders of the relationship's ending were blurry. It was my first serious relationship, and we were so determinedly in love. It didn't take too long for the both of us to fit into each others' lives, especially he in mine and my family's. For most of its duration, the relationship was easy, light and filled with ringing laughter. We were best friends, scurrying around on our own journeys, hoarding adventures and information to bring back to the other. But I think he and I had perhaps no way to tell the difference between being friends who were fond of each other, and being in love. But we thought we were for a good couple of years, before I suddenly, and overnight, found myself holding its crumbling pieces. When I looked up at him from the debris of our relationship, it was clear that he had known for a long, long time that we had ended.

And thus perhaps my toughest lesson:

Love was also two people in a well-meaning relationship experiencing two very different things, out of sync. Love, I learnt, was sometimes the ache of dissonance.

By the time I turned fifteen or sixteen, real life was just a tad out of my control. I had formed a close-knit circle of friends at school, but I also grew to be painfully awkward and shy. I was filling out into a body that didn't feel like mine and it was all happening (to all of us in class) in the presence of the opposite sex, which made it all the more horrific. Love was no longer on the menu, even as a means to kill time, because other things had started mattering more—what my body was doing, what it was not doing, and where I wanted my life to go next. So, in 2003, in a move that would perhaps set the tone for the coming decades of my life, and with the onset of a particular kind of technology that would change all our lives forever, I turned to the Internet.

For a kid who didn't feel like she belonged anywhere (and there truly was no permanent place to trace my roots), the Internet was home. After a quick initiation into the family computer and some MS-DOS games, right after the curve that took you down to censored porn town, I stumbled upon that glorious beacon for the hopeful and the horny, the Yahoo chat room. In a Linkin Park chat room, I found the love of my life, a sixteen-year-old called Andrew McFarland, who I didn't bother asking any other specifics for, because love is above things like details. We spoke on and off for a couple of weeks before he started disappearing for days together. I had asked him for a picture of himself before he disappeared, so when he resurfaced, it was one of the first things he sent. I got a small pixelated photo of the side profile of a pink-skinned man with bleached peroxide hair, who looked like he was straining really hard. You couldn't make out more because the photo was obviously cropped. 'It looks like you're in the middle of some exercise,' I replied to him over email, 'but you look just like Eminem LOL.' Andy disappeared again only to send me an email many weeks later to confess that he was, in fact, a forty-year-old man who wanted to connect with someone online. Andy wasn't even his name, obviously, and the picture I really liked of his was a crop from some porno he was watching. Love on the Internet was just like all of those things I had learnt from my experiences in real life, but much worse. It was a tough world for a naive fifteen-year-old whose favourite chat-room icebreaker was to ask people what their favourite planet was, because hers really was Uranus.

It'd take me at least another decade of cruising dating

websites to learn that there possibly was nothing there for me. Before I learnt that the temptation was always easy and insidious, because it promised a world of plenty where everyone else was just as lonely and hopeful as you were. Before I learnt that love was very, very complicated, and inextricable from your relationship with yourself.

A lifetime later, in 2019, we sold the house we stayed in for over fourteen years in Delhi. As part of the handover, we cleared out all the things we had hoarded in the small storeroom there—things too precious to survive the erosions of moving and time. One of these is a memory box in which, amongst other things, I had kept things gifted to me by the boys I had loved over the years. Handwritten cards, progress bar notes, a smooth stone with fossilized bird poop that looked like an 'S', anklets, keychains and a diary I wrote in from the ages of thirteen to seventeen. I crunched open the diary with its pages now clumping together until it split open to a page where, for some reason, I had a strip of unused Band-Aids.

I can't help but read poetry here, this small discovery of healing in a decaying herbarium of old loves.

Reading

Growing up as I did with an insatiable appetite for stories, my parents couldn't shovel them down my gullet fast enough for me. There was the added complication of them not being particularly conducive to bedtime storytelling. As if we were all adults simply cohabiting, they would spend time with me to my heart's fill during the day, but bedtime was personal. A big part of this had to do with Amma and Nanna's sleep routine during our early years as a family, when both of them worked. The minute their heads hit the pillow, they were out. Apart from a few sputtering, abortive missions in the art of oral storytelling from Nanna and Maamma, my stories were not read out, just read. (I wonder if that has any bearing on the fact that I learn best when I read something. No matter how deeply I'm listening, it doesn't settle into my mental webbings until I make a note of it.)

Thus it turned out that both Varun and I didn't really have a bedtime ritual of dozing off, heavy-lidded to the soothing lilt of an adult telling us a story. On Nanna's part, this wasn't for any lack of trying. The poor man seems to have been born with only a 2 kb document filed under 'Stories for Children'. After the first few nights of listening to the same two stories over and over, they were insufferable. He would try every tactic in the book (except actually pick up a book) to shake things up for us when we gently pointed out that we'd heard the story before. One was *Konga Nakka*, which was the old Aesop's fable *The Fox and the Crane* in Telugu. The other was an untitled outlier about a beggar who was blessed with gold coins by a fairy. As long as the jute sack he had could hold the coins in as the fairy poured them out of her wand, he could have as many as he wanted. If even one fell out of the bag, however, he would lose everything. We knew where this story would go. In his greed, the man would ask for one coin too many, which would slip out of the sack. To a cooing, gurgling babe, this story is about greed, a warning about not letting it get the better of you. But as I think of it over the years, I remain convinced it's really about the magical unicorn that is equitable wealth distribution under capitalism.

Amma, of course, always knew when to dignifiedly call it a day and explained to us early on that she'd be happy to read out stories from books but she wasn't going to sit and make them up in her head. This resistance to improvising stemmed from a great trauma that she had undergone when she had last improvised as a ten-year-old in her music class in school. As Young Padma belted out a note with some added flourish that she had heard from a song before, the teacher hurriedly motioned for the class to stop. As soon as she identified where the off-tune flourishes were coming from, the teacher pointed at Young Padma, snapping at her, 'You! Why are you croaking like a frog in the background?' That was the last time Padma improvised.

As chatty as I was, as hungry as I was for stories, my mother tells me I wasn't a demanding child. She'd buy me a book or hand me a magazine and even if I didn't know how to read yet and nothing made sense to me, I'd look at it for hours, keeping company as my mother read alongside me. Once, when I came home from kindergarten, Amma had a bright-yellow picture book on *Cinderella* for me, along with a Milton water bottle. This bottle had a sipper that was placed at the corner of the cap, as opposed to the more mainstream centre-capped ones. All the cool kids in my kindergarten had the side sipper. While I had admired them from afar, I hadn't registered the usual child-like need to want one for myself. I seemed to be content just marvelling at the bottles from afar. But clearly, I had waxed eloquent to Amma about them long enough for her to pick up on it. Just the gift of the book was amazing, a dopamine hit I would be particularly attuned to all my life, but reading with hydration? Priceless! I already knew the story of Cinderella, but it didn't matter—this was a new book, it demanded separate attention. I thus built during my formative years quite a complex dependency on books, like someone else might with food. Books were reward, books were solace, books were balm.

The first book that really made an impact on me was Louisa May Alcott's *Little Women*. I think it was an abridged version for young readers, and I remember it being illustrated, a compact hardcover that I liked tapping my nails on. It made me feel important. Alcott's book is a classic, and looks at the goings-on in the March family during the American Civil War, and focuses primarily on the four March girls—Meg, Jo, Beth and Amy. Beth's death was a watershed moment, in the book's narrative and in my own.

Beth is ill with scarlet fever, and is sick and bedridden for a long time. While she gets better with Jo tending to her, she eventually relapses and makes her peace with death. In a conversation she has with Jo, she asks them not to weep for her.

> I only mean to say that I have a feeling that it never was intended I should live long. I'm not like the rest of you. I never made any plans about what I'd do when I grew up. I never thought of being married, as you all did. I couldn't seem to imagine myself anything but stupid little Beth, trotting about at home, of no use anywhere but there.

A lot for an eleven-year-old to take in. Up until that moment, I hadn't thought of my life's purpose per se. I knew the things that interested me, and I had some inkling of what I'd like to be when I grew up, but what purpose did I serve, existing? Wasn't I a lot like Beth? Marriage had never entered my head; whatever little I had imagined my life to be was somehow by myself, and I couldn't for the life of me imagine much of my life. To my pre-teen self, it seemed to be a warning that I had to find a passion, or death would mark me. Without a passion I was an empty husk, and death would sift me away immediately from the kernel. I was highly interested in how the world worked, I never got bored easily and, yet, through my childhood, I assumed I would die at thirty because I could not envision life beyond it. It is a knot that remains in the pit of my stomach. As if to truly inhabit a space, you first have to create it by envisioning it. An eleven-year-old's belief that if I cannot imagine something, it must not exist.

Those of us who read most likely have a roster of the books that have impacted us. The ones that have left us gasping for air, out of delight, out of sorrow, out of shock. I chanced upon *The Old Man and the Sea* by Ernest Hemingway way before I was capable of understanding it. I may have been around eight, at most, an age where I assumed thin books quite obviously meant they were for children. I read the book in a couple of hours, bawling my eyes out but not exactly knowing why. All I could tell was that the book's beleaguered protagonist, Santiago, was old, and his life seemed very lonely and sad. I read it many years later and chuckled at my eight-year-old self: What *had* I gotten myself into? But I am moved still to note that even as a young reader who knew she was way out of her depth in a story, a book still somehow managed to relay the right blend of emotions, that even in the wilderness of comprehension, feelings were aplenty.

Another book that I read, well before *my* time at least (I do think it's subjective), was Arundhati Roy's *God of Small Things*. I don't remember how old I was, except that I was young enough to have missed the incest aspect of the storyline altogether. All the papers had been raving about her book and I didn't see what all the fuss was about. When I re-read the book (which I will argue was for all purposes my first reading), it was a whole new story. I learnt through both, the Hemingway and the Roy, that there is some such thing as the right time for a book, and, more importantly, the right pace.

Because I picked up reading early as a child, and read faster than average, I seemed to have learnt to read a book cover to cover. I may not have consciously thought about it, but it soon grew into a conditioning. As picture books turned to short abridged books turned to full-fledged novels, I found it harder and harder to stick to my old habit. But anything less than a one-sitting read was a failure on my part, and so I sat there in utter discomfort, trying to stuff myself with one page too many, lugging open-faced books along with me, stealing minutes during the course of my school days, trying to finish it in one go. Far from being enjoyable, reading books bordered on compulsion.

One of the first set of books my parents bought me was an anthology series called *Childcraft*. It was a set of around sixteen beautiful, illustrated hardcover books, along with an index and a dictionary, each covering a different theme. Book 4 was about endangered and extinct animals (*Nature in Danger*), where I learnt about the dodo; Book 7 (*The Universe*) triggered my lifelong fascination with planets and deep space. *Childcraft* was especially expensive in the early 1990s, and for whatever wild reason, even though they were both working overtime to make ends meet, my parents judged that the investment would be worth it, and I couldn't be more grateful. *Childcraft* was essential to how I viewed the world, what I thought children in other countries lived like, looked like. Years later, I dated someone who was the only other human I knew who had read *Childcraft* as a kid and thought it was sign enough from the Universe (both the literal one and Book 7) that he was the one. He wasn't, but it goes to show much I valued *Childcraft*'s presence in anyone's life. There were some used-book staples, such as the encyclopaedia for children *Tell Me Why?* and it's unimaginative sequel *Here's More...Tell Me Why?*, which I am sure I practically slept inside of. And as is mandatory reading for a middle-class urban child growing up in postcolonial India, Enid Blyton, who, unlike my parents, shovelled books down my gullet at thrice the speed at which I could consume them. It took years for me to get through her entire repertoire, and, embarrassingly, a few more to wake up to the subtle colonial racism sprinkled amidst the tongue, toffee and treacle. The journey after Blyton was not too far off the predicted path of adolescence—*Nancy Drew*, *Hardy Boys*, *The Baby-Sitters Club*, *Sweet Valley Twins*, *Goosebumps*; Judy Blume on this side of the bridge, and Robin Cook, Sidney Sheldon and Jeffrey Archer borrowed from my mother, on the other. I set up base in the middle of that bridge for a few years, until someone threw me J.R.R. Tolkein's *The Lord of the Rings* trilogy and I jumped off the bridge with it.

During my undergraduate years, I would spend hours in the library, graphing the dusty spines of mahogany library hardcovers with gold-embossed lettering with my fingers, hooking on to the ones that were at the point of utter dilapidation. I'd check them out and keep them at home, nursing them (only through, perhaps, sheer intention). Very soon, within the measly limits of what an undergraduate library card allows, I had an intensive care unit for neglected books in my room. Of those, I remember a particularly beat copy of George Orwell's *1984*, which I regularly checked out and renewed continuously for the three years of my degree. The spine was cracked in many places, threads coming out from the binding, the pages slowly splitting away from each other, so jaundiced from the years and from overexposure that they had become thinner, more translucent than butter paper. I performed multiple surgeries on the copy over those three years, holding the pages together with clear tape, spread after spread after spread. But I knew there wasn't much that could be done to make the book readable again, only these cosmetic tweaks that would hopefully keep it looking dignified until the end of its days. As dramatic and silly as it sounds, I squeezed in a tiny hug before returning it at the end of my degree, for the last time. Wheezing through its twilight days as it was, it had little to give me, and I understood that. Every book is a different animal. Even two copies of the same book, from the same print run, to me, hold a slightly different mood, a set of associations that is unique to it. I would go on to read *1984,* but it wasn't from that copy. I wonder if it still sits there, on one of the shelves of the English Literature section in the library at Kamala Nehru College, forced to somehow carry on in this life still—and if so, whether my suturing has eased the pain at all.

But, as fellow readers might also attest, reading is never just about books, is it? When you first start, plot is pleasure. You want to know what happens next, so you turn the page. If you like it enough, you'll probably stick to this habit. In a while you'll have turned so many pages, across so many genres and mediums, that the act of reading gets under your fingernails, your skin, the message in your synapses, between your neurons, until it is muscle memory, something deep inside of you, green and gnostic. You're always reading. It's you who are.

Tathaiyya, Amma's father, died of a heart attack when I was a little under two years old. Of the six grandchildren he had, I was the first, and the only one he saw. I am told Tathaiyya was absolutely smitten by me. By the time he was in his fifties, the pressure of being a parent had given way to the uncomplicated joy of being a grandparent. There was all this space for him to love and dote, without any of the exhaustion of caring for their futures in and out. My only memory of Tathaiyya is a very hazy one and, given that it happened when I was so young, perhaps one of my earliest ones too. And given how memory necessarily entropies, when I play it back now, I realize what I'm recalling is at best a memory of a memory. A facsimile memory. This is what I remember: I am sitting on Tathaiyya's chest, jumping up and down, and I am sure my curled-up baby fists are on his chest. I can't remember his face, none of his features are ever clear, but only that I sat on his chest—and something that happened two days later seemed to have stayed with me. I did not understand when everyone was mourning, and I didn't comprehend his death or loss, but a few years later, when Amma explained to me how Tathaiyya died, I immediately thought of that one memory and stood paralysed with fear that I had killed him. At first, I decided it would be best to not bring it up with the family, especially my maternal grandmother, Ammama. But the shame of death is too much for a stupid young girl, and in a moment of weakness, I found myself asking Amma for her forgiveness for killing her father. Although it both pained and puzzled Amma to hear what I was living with, she managed to gently explain to me that my memory had nothing to do with his death. The fists of a two-year-old simply could not stop a grown man's heart. My memory was real—I did play with Tathaiyya, and he did die the next day, but I had nothing to do with it. This hologramming, I learnt, is intrinsic to memory. You could remember the correct things, and remember them correctly, but, somehow, the sum total of your memory and its reading could still make it all incorrect.

My early days as a baby feminist in my undergraduate degree confirmed to me that you could indeed read *everything*. Once our professors taught us the art of gleaning things, we started seeing it everywhere. Everything was 'text'. Books, articles, songs, advertisements, jokes, application forms, your ex-boyfriend. Early into our first semester, one of my batchmates exclaimed, 'Oh god, ma'am, this can't go on. I can't stop analysing the power structures while watching *Tom and Jerry*!' Our professors assured us that this was perfectly natural, that our overwhelmedness was right on time. Soon we would discover, they maintained, that reading was a switch. The power was not in the reading, but in learning to discern when not to read. Our first lesson in feminism, it turned out, was self-protection.

Yet, as is often typical for introverts who've studied the humanities and read a lot, I've been told that I read too much into things. As if reading is an act that can and should be done only at a certain point, as if it were a veritable Yabukita cultivar of Japanese green tea that could be harvested only at a particular point in the plant's life. And even if you have made a reading of a situation, you shouldn't steep it for too long, or it becomes too bitter or acidic. I may have given it some consideration when I was younger, but I have grown to insist that reading (too much) into things is a political act. The things that alerted me to possibly unsavoury people or situations were because I read into them. So maybe there is some observational truth to women reading too much into things. But who decides what is too much? Whom does assessing and critically analysing hurt? Racism, sexism and other institutionalized systemic oppressions all wield this idea that you're simply overimagining slights, hyper-focusing on unintentional micro-aggressions and that we could all get along if you could just give humanism a chance. Over millennia, what women have been articulating as intuition or gut feeling is the power of reading—reading rooms, reading situations, the crowd, a group of men in an empty unlit alley at night, potential violence. Reading is painful, compulsive and unenjoyable, but I often wonder if we even have the luxury of switching off.

It's a delicate balance, this. Reading as resistance, not reading as protection, reading as protection, not reading as resistance. I'm learning to temper both these things now. To read for the joy of it (reading books, reading into things), to read and witness for the duty of it—and to know the difference. And perhaps this is the truth you have collected all those years putting word after word after word away, now wedged under your fingernails. That the ultimate purpose and reward of reading is discernment.

When I was young, Amma had pointed out a bunch of mynahs to me and taught me a rhyme. *One for sorrow, two for joy, three for a letter, four for a boy, five for silver, six for gold, seven for a secret never to be told.* The traditional rhyme goes up to ten, and is usually based on sightings of a magpie and portends that a single magpie by itself is bad luck. But Amma taught it to me by pointing at mynahs, and only remembered correctly until seven, and so seven became the base unit I operated with, not ten. An intergenerational game of telephone (or Chinese whispers, as it was more infamously and problematically called). Mynahs usually hang out in groups, so you're almost always going to find more than sorrow, and since I knew only up to seven, I would mentally divide large groups into sevens. Better yet, I soon realized, I could divide them into any number I wanted. Seven needn't be a secret, it could mean I was going to soon meet a boy and get a letter. Over the years, I manipulated the game even more, and in the event I caught only one mynah hopping along on a road, I'd read it as half-joy. There was no deception in this—if two mynahs made up joy, it was obvious that one would be half-joy. *One for half-joy, two for joy, three for joy and a half, four for twice*—the possibilities were endless. 'Where's your friend, buddy?' I'd ask a mynah catching a smoke break on my balcony ledge, 'Oi!

Go bring your friend along.' More often that not, she would usually be around somewhere. And if she wasn't, just the one was enough. Just the one was enough.

Years later, in a job interview for a university newspaper in Vancouver, I was asked what it was that I did besides reading and writing: 'Some of us here make videos, others have an interest in photography or cooking...what do you do outside of reading?' The question threw me off entirely; I'd never thought of it before. As I desperately listed off the things I loved doing in my head, I realized I didn't have any passions that weren't, at the core of it, reading. I gave them some underwhelming answer, I'm sure, and this might have had no bearing on the outcome, but I didn't get the job. The next few days, I tried rehearsing the question mentally, trying to perfect my answer for whenever I would be asked this next. Of course I enjoyed things outside of reading. In fact, towards the latter half of my twenties, my reading stamina had become pitiful. I hardly read any more. But...how come reading and writing weren't enough? More importantly, was that really all I had?

I always knew that while reading was my world, it didn't have to be everyone else's. The only other reader in my immediate family was my mother, and I think observing my father and brother taught me that people enjoyed spending time differently. I may have forgotten that during my years as a new literature student, any boy I was going to date had to read—it was the biggest deal-breaker. There is some poetic justice in the fact that none of my partners, long-term or fruitflies, have been readers. I don't think reading holds any superior social value in the scheme of hobbies any more. It does me good to remember that having books, having access to books, and having the time to read books for leisure are still marks of privilege.

On the other hand, as enjoyable as reading and writing could be for me, they were not unlike tics. Reading was a familiar, constant comfort and it was also the fastest way I knew to ingratiate myself into new schools, groups and friends. I read to learn, to process, to ache, to escape and to fit in. And perhaps it really is what comes to me the most naturally. Having been the new person for way longer than I have been 'one of the group', I assume I stick out like a sore thumb in all my classrooms, offices and friendships. I often visualize my moving as if I am standing on a planet, skipping across it, faster and faster, until the centripetal force of the momentum gives me a lift-off, levitates me, always just in orbit of these communities that I join and form intimate bonds with, but almost always as if I am an embedded journalist, who will eventually go back and report on these places. Always just a little outside of the moment.

Like a younger me wrote in her diary once, through the dense thicket of teenage years, *'There are some circles you will get into. For everything else, there's a book.'*

Flesh

In another life, my body is not dragging me through a war of its own making. In that life, I am in control of my mind and body as one unit, seamless and efficient. But it is always this life, the one that is afforded to us. In this one, I desperately wish for a body that doesn't make its fragility so openly known. Like a child misbehaving in a supermarket aisle who somehow knows the power of witness, it makes a spectacle, and I stand next to it, an embarrassed parent, placating, bribing, adjuring it to remember what we had decided, what I had taught it, to not do it here, not like this, in front of everyone. And yet, how easily it reveals its cracks for the whole world to see, how eager it always is for acknowledgement.

With my chronic illness flaring up majestically in my twenties, I was almost always hurting. Folks with chronic illnesses, especially invisible ones, learn quickly to stop articulating these pains and discomforts. When you realize that you're in some kind of pain more days than not, you stop articulating your aches. In how many ways does one articulate the normal? With some amount of deftness, I've learnt to assess the state(s) of my body daily, first thing in the morning and often during the day, before filing it away. Assess, don't articulate.

Friends have sometimes looked at me in both disbelief and pity. 'How can one person be sick in so many ways?' They think they're keeping the thought to themselves, but you can sense it in the air when you're with them—the very density of the room changes. Like an osmotic fluid, it always leaks out. I understand how this happens. There is a limited bandwidth afforded to each of us, and there's only so many times you can vocalize discomfort or disease before there's a switch that goes off in your listener's brain. And sometimes, that listener is yourself. Saturated with the dysfunctions of your body, you stop forming the words to name them. By refusing to name these aches daily, I snap their power in half, take away their bite.

After the flare-up at the end of 2018, which had me move back home for help in Delhi, we visited doctors, worried it was undiagnosed mental illness that I was merely assuming was depression and anxiety. One of those doctors diagnosed me with severe depression and prescribed two sets of pills. Another thought it was a minor panic disorder.

No one's listening. I am constantly asked to tell them 'the

other stuff'. 'Don't say depression or anxiety. Don't use those words. Tell me all of this again without those words. No, it cannot be your birth control. No one really reacts that much to it, even if you have PCOS. Tell me what else is bothering you.' There is no other stuff, it is always this PCOS stuff, but no one's listening.

A few weeks and three doctors later, my GP asks me to take a few blood and hormone tests. Everything that can be low is horrifically low. My GP calls me the second the reports are in. 'No wonder you've been feeling so dissociative and detached. These deficiencies affect your neural health and memory-making capacity. I'm surprised you even remember what happened yesterday.' Blood reports show that my neuroses are, in fact, quite rooted in the physical—low vitamins, low iron, borderline hypothyroidism, amongst a litany of older, more familiar culprits.

I'm not sure what triggered this clusterfuck, and cannot trace it to any one moment. When you're flying a plane, they say, each degree matters. One degree might not seem much of an angle or a difference to the immediate eye, but one degree off course can land your flight to a different city, country or continent. I wonder if my recent symptoms were my body's way of alerting me to some faulty cog in my works, and I confidently dismissed those signals, pushing on regardless.

Pushing on is a habit I picked up over the latter half of my twenties, and I have assumed over the years a stance of tough love. Cancelling plans last-minute because of slow-building or sudden flare-ups gains you a reputation amongst friends, and at first you try laughing along with them as they joke about it, before understanding that because you stopped articulating your illness(es) and naming them, no one remembers you're not like them. They chalk it up to laziness, some kind of moral paucity that makes you a tardy human, disrespectful of others' time. It's not really anyone's fault because you've deluded yourself too that your body is like anyone else's. So I push through 'bad' or 'low' days more than I indulge them. Because of how exhausting it can be to navigate social life around chronic illness (especially when you look perfectly fine to everyone else), I often overcompensate by refusing to check in with my body. I have manually overridden my systems to push through so often, and for so long, that doing the exact opposite of what I 'feel' I need to has become the prescribed course correction.

How much of a person is outside of their body? Like a delicate chemical experiment, how much of Shruti is this specific amount of Vitamin D, that specific ratio of oestrogen to progesterone, this exact amount of insulin in the blood, these precise hours of deep sleep?

In Chennai, I register new pains, unrelated to the otherwise daily swings of my syndrome. By now, I usually know what depressive symptoms feel like; I notice when I slowly start disengaging from social media, when I don't have the energy to respond to people checking in on me (*I stopped having energy to initiate conversations a long while ago*). I know what to do when I sense an anxiety attack building. But almost for over a year now, I have started feeling dissociated from everything, I blank out when someone asks me what I did two days ago and embarrassingly forget important updates in my friends' lives. I try getting my sleep cycle on track, meditate, exercise, but through it all, the uneasy feeling stays. This new companion is quiet, insidious and comes with its own set of throbbing pains. Small injuries take forever to heal, a sciatic nerve flare-up pulses in rage through the day.

Oddly, for someone who has struggled with weight through her twenties, I am the fittest and lightest I've ever been. In the middle of this building dread and despair, I have found the discipline to lose 12 kg. I hold on to this corner of my life like a life jacket that keeps me bobbing up and down as everything else sinks. After years of struggling with fitness and weight because of PCOS, I have finally got something right, and hold on to it with obstinacy. This is the most important act of kindness I can perform for myself, especially if I end up living by myself for the rest of my life. I am disappearing physically, which eases so many of my chronic symptoms, and gives me the only stability I have during my day. I am light on my feet, my lungs can now expand to give me the deepest breaths I've taken, but it's not long before this weightlessness becomes dizzying.

By the time I'm recovering from this mental-health episode, I'd wager I'm more the things outside of my body. I am now wholly defined by a lack of. And so I have to find my elements slowly, one vitamin injection, one deep breath, another biotin supplement and probiotic drink at a time, assembling myself through these medical horcruxes.

Growing up, the sense I got from my parents was that things to do with the naked body, our very flesh, weren't necessarily something one spoke about. This wasn't a censoring—my parents answered any questions I had as a child with patience and fortitude, knowing that one answer just meant more probing questions. The idea was that the body was an instrument that did things that not everyone needed to know about. Perhaps one or two steps ahead of shame, and one or two steps behind comfort. Amma and Nanna answered my questions where my friends' parents wouldn't, but these were still slightly uncomfortable conversations, carried out only by bullheadedness. As a result, I don't remember being hyper-curious about what each of us covered with clothes every day, as much as I was given to assuming that there was nothing there to see. Even through this ideological pixelation of the human body, I seemed to have picked up the threads of shame.

I was around ten when one evening, Amma called out from the kitchen, asking us all to come and eat dinner. Nanna had gone to take a bath, so Amma asked me to quickly check if he was out yet, and if so, to let him know that dinner was ready. I trotted into their bedroom, dark but for the square brackets of thin white light bordering the bathroom door. Just as I was about to yell out to Amma that he was still taking a bath, Nanna opened the door.

Accounts from people who have had intensely spiritual or near-death experiences, or from folks reporting on their experience with psychotropic drugs like DMT, often mention 'a tunnel of light'. There seems to be a commonality in what this tunnel of light entails. People mention feeling like they are floating through a dark tunnel before being ejected into a dimension that has a brilliant, blinding whiteness. Now, granted my experience cannot be argued to be either near-death or a drug trip, but it was, all the same, life-changing. I had floated into a dark room, unprepared for the white blinding light of the bathroom, confronted with the visage of my father who, still unaware of my presence, had stepped out in his briefs.

While I stood frozen in fear next to the door, unsure of how to make my escape, a tinny sound escaped my mouth. My father was suddenly alerted to my presence in the room. Revealed at once, and so unexpectedly, I startled like a mouse and made a beeline for my room, scattering pathetic 'sorry's across my trail of shame. Amma saw me scurry to my room and called out to everyone again. 'Come eat!' If only my poor mother knew, I thought to myself as I entered our room. A few seconds later, she called out to me again. 'Awfully sorry for this, my dear, but I'm afraid I'm in a bit of a spot,' I wanted to say to her, 'and I'll be needing all your smelling salts.' This poor innocent woman, providing for her family, ignorant of the fact that her daughter had just done the unthinkable. And although there was no manual to running a family that we were all reading out of, the rules of family life seemed clear to me. I had seen my father in his underwear and now I had to leave the family. My journey here had come to an end and I had to hang my my apron, snuff my torch. It was time for me to go.

I stood in my room for a quick second, trying to catch my breath and survey what to pack first and where I could possibly go from there. Would my school be sympathetic to my plight? Perhaps our curmudgeonly downstairs neighbour, old-lady-Aboody, would take me in. Although, given that she regularly hit her ceiling with a stick to indicate her displeasure at Varun and my shenanigans, combined with the fact that she hated us, one could not be sure. I suddenly regretted all the times I had sneezed towards the floor, hoping the virus would soak through the concrete separating us and that she'd get my cold.

Amma called out to me one last time, using The Voice. My window of escape had narrowed down to the breadth of a needle. I had to walk out and face the elimination.

I sheepishly stepped out of my room and saw Nanna walk towards our kitchen (fully clothed, for those keeping track) and braced myself for the worst. He was obviously going to reveal my transgressions to Amma. Oh god, did this mean I had to leave behind the books that Varun and I shared? Did I have to leave my clothes behind because, technically, my parents had bought it with their money? Ugh, there were so many calculations to be done, and I was racing against the clock. I heard the clink of laughter from the kitchen and felt a tinge of sadness. Goodbye Amma, goodbye family, sorry I couldn't spend more time with you. I took my seat at the table, head down, next to a clueless Varun playing what I could only empirically observe to be a game of 'car crash' with his Hot Wheels.

My parents came out of the kitchen and took their seats. Nanna started serving everyone. I was sure he was not going to put any food on my plate. He did. Oh, I see. They were going to soften the blow. But I knew it would come eventually. I was ready. Except, of course, you know where this story is going. Nothing happened. Absolutely nothing happened! My parents continued their conversation, pausing regularly to check in with Varun and me about the state of our food, and Varun was, at this point, driving one Hot Wheels car directly inside the pile of rice on his plate. Everything was like it was before. I had seen my father in his underwear and the world hadn't ended.

When I tell him this story years later, it's clear that my father hadn't even realized I was in the room, or even if he had at the time, it was so very little out of the ordinary that it hadn't qualified to make it to his long-term memory cache. It's not like there was anything to ignore or sweep under the carpet, there was just nothing for my father to address. So just like it had built up in my head, the great scandal of flesh also came crumbling down. People had bodies made of flesh, and that was that. It would be a while before that scandal built up again, but that was an inevitable rite of passage for a bunch of pre-teens who secretly passed around the *Oxford Dictionary* in class with the entries to 'Sex' and 'Breasts' dog-eared beyond belief.

In fifth standard, Kritika invited the girls in our section to her birthday party. It was one of our first 'cool' parties—it was on the day of our last exam, so as soon as school ended around noon, we all huddled into her car and were driven to her flat in Cuffe Parade. All of us had brought our change of clothes along and took turns using her bathroom to dress up. We all went downstairs and hung out in the apartment complex's main garden, which was deserted but for us. A friend noticed scraps of paper on the grass and picked one of them up. 'Oh my god!' she yelled at us excitedly, and we ran over mid-gossip to gather around the paper she held up. And there it was—one half of the human boob in all its naked glory. Someone else noticed the other scraps and we collected them and pieced them together on the grass. It was clear that this was from some soft-porn brochure of a magazine, the girl wore some kind of a cheap version of a latex suit, with her breasts exposed, except for a thin cane crossed across it, hiding nothing. We quickly looked around us to see if anyone in the garden or in the buildings encircling the garden had noticed what we'd done. Our excitement soon changed to fear and we tried scattering the scraps just like we had found them. It must have been a sight to someone watching from a distance. Five or six pairs of spindly limbs randomly kicking at grass. Once we were satisfied with our rearrangement, we scooted the hell out of there and hurried back up to Kritika's house. The rest of the evening we sat in her room, watching TV, but none of us could talk about anything but that image. Why would anyone agree to appear topless in a magazine? What if their parents saw it? Why would any man want to see a woman like that? Was that what our boobs were going to look like? Who was looking at that photograph anyway, and why did they leave it there in a children's park, so easy for a child to pick up?

The age at which I had gathered that something like porn existed on the Internet (twelve) coincided beautifully with the arrival of the first public computer in the Rao household. As soon as I could make my way around the Internet, I remember gingerly dipping my feet in the ocean that was Google, hesitantly asking it to find entries for 'sex' or 'boob'. Ah, the primal high of your one designated hour of the week on the Internet, hearing your modem make that high-pitched, clicking mating call and offering you websites with naked people with golden stars censoring their genitals. One day I decided to raise the stakes and directly enter a website in the menu bar—if I remember correctly, it was something as vapid as 'sex.com'. (According to the *Oxford Dictionary* being floated around in our fifth-standard classroom, this was the Word of the Year). It was a top-notch experience, except for the fact that no one had told me about Internet cache and search history. This minor detail was revealed to me one day as I happened to stand behind Nanna when he was checking his email. As my father painfully typed out every alphabet with one finger on the keyboard, I noticed to my horror that the menu box dropped down with the closest options. Since there were some two websites all of us put together visited, sex.com was not far down that list. I was about to shit my pants. Thankfully, Nanna hadn't learnt typing on a keyboard yet, not without looking intently at the keyboard anyway, so he dutifully typed out hotmail.com and life went back to normal. I thought I'd dodged a bullet. But a week or so later, my mother called me, saying she wanted to talk to me about something serious. I sat in front of her on the floor of her room, and she said, 'Nanna and I noticed that there was a bad-sounding website on our Internet. And it can come only if one of us has gone there. So…'

    I was quick to dispel any fire, especially before my father walked into the room. 'I reaaaally wouldn't know, Amma, although I must say I do share your horror. We can't take this lightly.' Amma saw that I was not going to bite easily.

'Varun's too young and doesn't even use the computer; it's just the three of us and it sure as hell isn't me…' she said. The eagle indeed had a sharp eye and she was circling in on me. This was not a moment for weakness. So I dodged.

Like a champ, I immediately responded with, 'Agreed, and I know it isn't me either, so…'

'Are you…saying…your father…is logging on to sex.com?' Amma asked, pausing deliberately through the sentence to emphasize the incredulousness of what I had suggested. Clever move, because I was clearly going to sign my name off on that statement if I confirmed the above.

'I mean I'd love to know too, but I really can't speak for him,' I said and left the room. Amma never pursued it again and I quickly learnt how to delete history. I don't suppose Amma ever told him about my brazened bulldozing of his image, because years later, when I recounted the story, my father looked at me hurt. 'Wow, you'd really throw me under the bus like that?!'

By the time Varun entered that phase, my parents had learnt to let go of battles they couldn't control. 'At least he's learning his spellings,' my father said with a desperate optimism in his voice, looking at me and Amma for confirmation.

Feeling betrayed by or dissonant with my body was something I experienced even when I was really young. I started bed-wetting around the time Amma was hospitalized for her miscarriage, and it would last on and off through the years, ending when I was around eleven or twelve. It seemed wholly out of my control at the time, no matter how hard I willed myself to not let it happen. I tried going to sleep praying or chanting 'No pee! No pee!', visualizing a tap being turned off tightly, or thinking intently of the dry Sahara desert I had read about in one of my *Childcraft* books. And yet, in spite of all of this, I would bed-wet frequently in my younger years. So as far back as I can remember, I was acutely aware of how my body could do things outside of my conscious control. Even now I can conjure up the welts of humiliation pulsing across my face when I'd wake up, and much before I'd see the wet bed sheet, before I could register the dampness I was sleeping in, I would see Amma standing next to me, so very exasperated, hurrying me off the wet bed and out of my wet clothes. In a few minutes I'd be dry and warm again, and even though Nanna would always make it a point to come to let me know it was okay, I remained completely ashamed of what my body was doing.

Amma's sister is married to Nanna's brother, that dramatic case of siblings marrying into the same family. Because of this incredibly minimal degree of separation in the family tree, and in spite of growing up across continents, both families have always been quite close to each other. During one of our combined summer vacations in Hyderabad, I discovered that my cousins, Sharat and Priya, had a song that my aunt and uncle would sing to them during bedtime. It was a well-known Hindi classic sung by Kishore Kumar, called *Aa Chalke Tujhe*. The song is melodious, breezy and the lyrics are like a hot shower hitting that one spot on the back of your neck. It would put my cousins to sleep successfully. Everyone in our extended family knew this to be a thing. Sharat and Priya had a family song—their song. I most certainly was envious of this explicit show of affection, this gentle ushering to sleep. Here, in the Rao household, the closest we would come to a family song was a popular morning bop called 'Oh come on! Who wet the bed again?' (always me).

Varun might have wet the bed once or twice in his life, but I dragged him into my one-person bed-wetter's club and projected a life where the both of us routinely watered the bed, so to speak. Sometimes, if I woke up immediately after the accident in the middle of the night, I would try rolling Varun towards the puddle to hide my tracks and deflect blame. Needless to say, it never worked. To rub this in my face even more, Varun would perform his brotherly duty by giving our common friends a short tour of our room when they visited, pausing for a second at my Lake of Shame. 'The bed sheets are off because they're drying in the balcony. See this dried puddle mark here? That's where Shruti peed last night, again.'

As questionable as a lot of my actions were as a child, I retain a little affection for the younger me, especially when I remember that I would immediately react with exaggerated horror to Varun's revelation but never denied it. I remain so grateful for the fact that even in our cruellest moments with each other, Varun never brought my bed-wetting up to shame me. To him—my closest friend, roommate, the person I spent the most time with—the bed-wetting was a matter of fact.

While Varun and I would joke about it, and Nanna would comfort me, Amma remained tight-lipped. I used to fear her reaction the most, because it was a studied non-reaction. I read disappointment, disgust and exasperation in her body language, but as an adult, I can't be sure who those feelings really emanated from—was it her or me?

From the comforts of temporal separation from that phase, I now think Amma wasn't disgusted as much as she was bone tired of having to air out a double-bed mattress in the sun every other day. While she may not have said anything to me when I wet the bed, neither comforting nor condemning, she would immediately change my bedding and clothes—she kept me dry. This is her language of love, I have to remember. She speaks it differently.

To curb its occurrence, my parents would regularly ask me every night if I had gone to the bathroom before sleeping. During sleepovers at friends, my parents would either ask before they left me there, or make it a point to call me up at night to ask if I had emptied my bladder. Dutifully I would say yes, irrespective of whether I had or not. Miraculously, I never wet the bed in someone else's house, so I suppose my body still was capable of getting its act together through sheer will. But at home, with family, my trickery of tongue never worked. Overnight, my body would tell on me. Decades later, it is still how I describe having a chronic illness that manifests outwardly in very cosmetic symptoms—my body tells on me.

Weight is still something that is gendered, and often considered by society at large to be a 'female' topic. It is seen as a natural womanly obsession, to constantly calibrate how much space you take up and, more importantly, are seen as taking up. I soon realized, however, that irrespective of where I stood with my weight, it didn't stop others from weighing in. When it comes to the weight on our bodies, we're all always projecting. Too thin, too fat, too fit, healthy but too obsessed. I've had friends anoint me as plus-size, chubby and just-a-few-kilos-overweight to 'oh you're absolutely fine'. Sometimes (most times) these opinions were unasked for, but, you see, this wasn't really about me. It was always an act of also reassuring *themselves*. Either that they were better off than me, or that we were healthy or unhealthy, fine or aching *together*. When people have tried to make sartorial decisions for me, they've either bought clothes a couple of sizes smaller or a few sizes larger than what I wore, and it is such an interesting exercise. This is how much space *they* think I take up.

It's still socially acceptable for celebrities in every sphere to talk about their weight or diet, but where are the women talking about body hair? Or possible balding? Horrible acne? Where's my *Cosmo* story about a female celebrity performing an emergency chin-hair plucking in her powder room? Amidst the various debilitating effects of my hugely prevalent syndrome, there are only two we talk about in the open. Weight and infertility. The intricate rules of gender performance continue to carve their effects on the bodies of young girls. I spent so many years trying to read up as much as I could on PCOS, only to have most resources circle back to infertility or obesity. To be sure, these are problematic symptoms, and a lot of folks with PCOS suffer from one, or both. But it drove home the point to a young twenty-year-old that her body did not matter until she made it look appealing, or it realized its purpose.

I'm sure that if it wasn't PCOS, I would have grappled with other passing comments or concerns. We police bodies wantonly, female bodies in particular. By now I have a compendium of other passing comments I've preserved over the years, carefully analysed, labelled and archived in plastic so it has a shelf life of forever, to be opened on days when self-flagellation is quite the theme of the night. And perhaps, like in the case of many women before me, some of the cruellest shaming has come from doctors.

I started my period a few months shy of turning thirteen. Amma and I walked to a public phone booth in our colony market and called Ammama to relay the news. I stood next to Amma as she excitedly told my grandmother that I had had my first period, that my body had passed the biological test. And even though I had desperately wanted my period to start so that I could level up to the other girls in my class, this announcement was a bit too overboard, even for me. Amma handed me the phone so that Ammama could congratulate me. I thanked her. She promised to gift me something special for this moment. In hindsight, I feel like we may have called it a little early, because I never had a timely period again. It either came late, or skipped the month entirely. No one paid much attention to it at first, and patiently waited for my hormones to settle.

By 2009, by the time I was twenty, something was deeply wrong with my uterus. After nine years of irregular periods and sudden, almost overnight weight gain, Amma and I realized I should probably go to a doctor. At the same time, a friend in my undergraduate class first used the term 'Polycystic Ovary Syndrome' in a conversation we were having about her health. Her symptoms were slightly different from mine, but common enough for me to make a note of the syndrome's name to research later. 'My doctor says it's because women are trying to be men these days. They drink like men, smoke like men, and work as many hours as them to prove they are equals. This throws the delicate energy of the female body off. It's apparently how I have PCOS,' she told us. I considered her doctor's logic for a moment, and even in my absolute illiteracy towards the syndrome, sussed that it was probably the doctor's intellectual energy that was off.

Regardless, I went home that day and looked up 'Polycystic Ovary Syndrome', and recognized a lot of what I had thought were previously unconnected symptoms. I was chronically fatigued, constantly craving starch and processed carbs, and my periods were always late, which made my PMS last for weeks. Amma and I decided to visit a doctor yet again. The first time I brought up my symptoms with my GP, I was around sixteen. He asked me to wait a couple of months and see if the irregularities would settle on their own. 'It takes a couple of years for the menstrual cycle to regularize. These are teething menstrual issues,' he wagered. I started my period nine years ago, I thought to myself—which nine-year-old is still teething?

A family friend who was a doctor suggested we get an ultrasound done. If I had cysts (small undeveloped follicles) lining my ovaries, that could be confirmation of PCOS. And so Amma and I walked over one day to a pathology lab next to our house, asking independently for a pelvic ultrasound, despite having a doctor who ideally should have asked for it first. I drank about 3,000 litres of water and asked my mother to roll me down the hallway like a barrel into the sonography room. I hoisted myself up on the table-bed contraption, a jiggling water balloon about to burst at the slightest touch. 'So lucky that we got this without prior appointment,' Amma said to me, just as the doctor walked into the room.

One look at him and I knew who he was. I frequented the neighbourhood gym every day and he was every gym-goer's nightmare. I was stumped. In the gym, the man was obnoxious. He'd chat loudly on his phone all through his casual stroll on the treadmill, every now and then wiping the phone screen on his headband. Everyone tried steering clear of him when he approached the weights, because he'd grunt loudly and make a show of doing any exercise at all. To top it all, despite wearing a headband and a wristband to keep the sweat off, he would swipe his index finger on his forehead and flick beads of sweat in a spectacular projectile motion across the sticky wooden floor of the gym. If there was a Buzzfeed quiz called 'What Kind of Gym-Goer Are You?', his ideal outcome would be, 'Alpha Mouth-Breather: Honestly, you should be banned.' Because this was a modest gym with no music playing, everyone brought their own music, except for when this gent spoke to the woman who was not his wife. It must be made clear that the knowledge of his extramarital affair required zero deduction from the rest of us. He would be talking sweet nothings to someone, only to abruptly say something like, 'Hold on, my wife's on the other line, I'll just call you back.' None of us cared about what the fellow did in his private life, we just didn't want it dumped on us every day, along with his spittle and sweat. I worried for a second that he might recognize me. But, because he was so consumed by the goings-on in his own life, he hardly bothered to register his surroundings, and therefore, it came as no surprise that he didn't recognize me.

I tried not to visualize his face dripping with sweat as he loomed over me to apply the gel for the ultrasound. A couple of questions later, he pulled up a livestream of my uterus on the screen. I obviously could not make out anything because, for one, the screen was behind my head, so the only view I had was of the doctor. My mother sat a few feet away, right behind him, an audience of one subjected to my entry at the Debutante Ball for Dysfunctional Ovaries.

'You should show this to your doctor, of course,' he said as he peered deeply into my uterus, broadcast on the screen like *Jaani Dushman* on Zee TV, 'but, in my opinion, this is a clear-cut case of PCOS.' Even though I was relieved to hear this somewhat-official diagnosis, another realization crept up on me. The doctor and I have now been bonded by a weird intimacy. I knew his deep secret and now he knew mine. 'Nothing to worry about,' he told my mother as I rolled my way to the bathroom, 'she just needs to lose weight and she'll be fine. When she needs to plan to conceive, you can deal with it then.'

It was probably an unwise thing to do, dear reader, but we listened to the radiologist. We trusted that all medical advice was standardized and so I let it go, too full with the giddiness, the relief of diagnosis to even begin to consider what one does with an illness post its naming.

In another few years, by 2012, my PCOS symptoms worsened. I had been losing and putting on the same few kilos, but coupled with the stress of moving cities, starting my first job at a daily newspaper and having a long-term relationship unexpectedly end (for me), I started having periods that were, on an average, twelve days long. I still didn't visit a doctor for my PCOS, holding on to the radiologist's advice that all I needed to do was be fit again. I had brought myself to this place, I could be the only one to get myself out of it. When my aunt visited me in Pune, she suggested we visit a gynaecologist she knew.

My aunt and I sat face to face with the gynaecologist in her small, cozy clinic. After a few pleasantries, the doctor asked me if I'd like for my aunt to leave the room so I could talk freely. I told her that it was fine, that I'd be happy to answer all questions in front of my aunt. After asking me about my lifestyle habits and symptoms, she quickly glanced at my aunt before asking me, with concerted nonchalance, 'Okay...and are you having an affair?'

'I've been dating someone for the last three years...' I offered, a little confused.

'No, no. That's all fine. But is it an affair?'

'No...?' I sputtered, looking desperately at my aunt for help.

'See...you have to tell me if you are having an affair because that will change whether you should go for a transvaginal ultrasound or not.'

It slowly dawned on me that 'having an affair' was some kind of code for having sexual intercourse.

'Oh! No! I am not having an affair,' I said to her, resolutely. I didn't know it then, but I was in a relationship with someone who indeed was having an affair, but that was beside the point. She squinted. 'Are you sure? You can't lie about this.'

'I'm really not having an affair,' I maintained. Whether she determined if I was lying or not (I wasn't), she finally let it go.

Before she prescribed any course of treatment, she asked me to lay on the doctor's table for a general check-up. I lay on my back and took deep breaths as she checked for my vitals. Applying pressure on my torso to check for organ health, she commented on the fat on my stomach. Just as I was about to get up from the bed, she pinched a chunk of my stomach between her index finger and thumb. 'See this?' she said and, before I knew it, slapped my breast. 'This is all just fat. This is what has to go.'

I felt dirty and violated in the moment, even though I knew that in the doctor's head, this was perfectly acceptable 'tough love', especially to a patient of the same sex. I measured this violation against the battles I was already fighting by then, and out of self-protection, let it go. For the first time in my life, I was prescribed oral contraceptive pills, with zero insight on why I needed it or how long I'd need to take it. Nothing about what the possible side-effects of the pills would be, or whether that was the best course of treatment for me at all. Even the possibility of having a conversation, where I could ask her questions about PCOS, about *my* PCOS, was foreclosed to me. She also threw in a specific protein powder that I had to buy off her and use as meal replacement. The bottle looked like it had been made in someone's basement.

It was a good lesson. That inside a doctor's office, you are sometimes just a set of symptoms. And it's not because you didn't try to vocalize your illness. Sometimes, the doctor is busy looking through you, assuming that whatever comes out of your mouth is a deception and is thus trying to get to the bottom of the facts, in spite of you.

By the time I was twenty-seven and leaving for my second master's in Vancouver in 2015, I met an endocrinologist in Mumbai. Aside from my usual symptoms, which would go through phases of normalizing and then disarray, I started noticing that I was consistently losing a lot of hair, and whatever hair remained on my head was thinning. By then, PCOS was firmly in the public eye. Newspaper articles frequently reported on its prevalence, YouTube channels specific to PCOS popped up regularly and almost every other friend I knew seemed to have it. Medical rhetoric also seemed to indicate that PCOS might be more of an endocrinological issue, not a gynaecological one. So I went to someone who was well known for working with women with PCOS. He was slightly older than the all the doctors I had gone to before, and seemed to be really engaging and kind when we first met him. Over the course of the three appointments I was to have with him, though, I realized he was thoroughly paternalistic, and thought any sound coming out of my mouth was as good as static between television channels.

In my first consultation, he checked my weight and body-fat percentage and let me know that I had the metabolic age of a fifty-four-year-old woman. 'Isn't this scary,' he asked me with a patronizing smile. 'You're the same age as your mother!'

He put me on a combination of an anti-androgen pill, a progesterone pill, a pill to manage insulin and a hair-growth serum. 'But this is not going to do anything until you lose weight, okay? You seem like an intelligent girl, you need to start investing in yourself. Why did you stop caring for yourself?' he asked. The condescending attempt at poignancy really pissed me off, but I assumed that my personal feelings towards the doctor needn't mar my professional trust in him. I started taking the pills and was soon reeling from the collective side-effects. Apart from asking me to get a liver profile test done every three months to see if I could tolerate the dosage of anti-androgen, I was not told about any of the side-effects of these pills. I spent the five months before leaving for Vancouver feeling faint and nauseous all the time. I hardly slept because my sleep was disturbed so often, and my stomach felt like it had a constant slow-burning fire. My breasts ached so badly that it hurt to move. I couldn't toss in my bed without crying out from pain. When I went back to the doctor to tell him about the side-effects, all he had to offer was that I'd be so much prettier if I just lost some weight, and I should choose to invest in myself, even if it meant tolerating all this pain.

Just before I left for Vancouver, I shared with him that I was going to be writing my thesis on PCOS in India, especially how the medical community talked to patients (and each other) about it. He congratulated me, and offered his resources if I ever needed them. Towards the end of our appointment, he asked my mom to step out of the room because he needed to talk to me alone. Despite my insistence that I was okay with her being there, he requested that she leave. Once it was just the two of us, he said to me conspiratorially, 'When you're in Canada, watch out for women who are overfamiliar with you. They might seem like they are helping you out, but this is how lesbians make their move. Once you're obliged to them for their help, there's no escape.'

Although I took six months' worth of medication with me, I stashed them in a drawer and never opened it. Before leaving Vancouver, I threw them all out with the trash. I never went back to the doctor again, even when I moved back to Mumbai two years later. Although a visit to a doctor's clinic is supposed to work on cold hard empirics of diagnoses and lab results, it is always, I learnt, always a moral diagnosis first.

At the age of twenty-nine, back in India, I went to another gynaecologist this time. All through my time in Vancouver, being 'unmedicated' for my PCOS, my periods had stretched to thirty- to forty-five-day-long blurs. I had started feeling a lot more zoned out, and my depressive episodes lengthened. When I moved back to India, with a publishing job in hand in Chennai, I knew I couldn't handle all of this stress on my own, and decided to see another doctor. I knew chances were he'd put me on the oral contraceptive pill, and it's exactly what I wanted. I wanted my body to just shut up for a second, to clear my head. In passing, I mentioned the severe side-effects I had had with my previous medication, and the doctor asked what my dosage for the anti-androgen was. 'No wonder you were feeling so fried,' he told me. 'This is ten times the dosage I would consider apt.'

He prescribed a birth-control pill and assured me that if I were to have any major side-effects with it, it would manifest in the first few weeks or months. This was untrue, but I would have no other way to know until the effects snowballed well out of my control. I was told to keep a close eye on my moods and cycles for the first couple of days, and everything seemed fine then. I had 'regular' periods that ended in five or six days and I could now track my period month to month. My skin wasn't chaffed from prolonged wearing of pads and I didn't have months-long PMS symptoms. For the first time in my life, I stopped carrying sanitary pads on me every day of the year, and there was a date on a calendar that validated my normalcy. But as I would soon find out, because my doctor skipped telling me, this was all a hormonal simulation, and I was just buying time.

When you are so dissonant with your body, how do you ask for love? With what strength do you put your humiliation aside to ask someone else to touch you or hold you? Once you manage to do that, can you tell them to understand somehow that this is your body, yes, but that your jurisdiction over it is sometimes hazy? Can you explain to them that intimacy with you is a game of Minesweeper—that they'll have to pay close attention to where their fingers go? If they manage to touch you without setting your embarrassment off, there are always adjacent grids on your body, primed to explode. You can't touch my chin, you can't place your hand on my stomach, don't look at my body too much, especially not under sunlight, just please be drunk so you won't notice anything, or if you do, please don't remember it when you're sober. Each time you guide their hand (always away from certain places, you've never had the bandwidth to find out where pleasure is), you think of people who genuinely have no care, or have worked towards having none, those who have learnt to be unashamed of their bodies. You think of how much more enjoyable it would be for your partner to be with them instead. You catch yourself thinking of how much more of a relief it would be for *you* if they were with someone else instead. Desperate to bring something to the table, you decide that the only way to win at this game is to forfeit it. So you overcompensate by learning how to make your partner feel happy and good. You deflect, deflect, deflect. Pretty soon your wiring changes and like a parasitic root that lives off its host, your only pleasure comes from knowing you get your partner off. They don't mind this setup. No one ever tells you that your shame is not unfounded. There is no immaculate conception.

That this is a game setup and created entirely by me is a different matter, and by so closely associating hair and fat and stubble and imperfection with shame, I've rigged it so that the house always wins. I always feel shame. I've walked into relationships with partners all through my twenties truly believing I was held hostage, that they could save me by releasing me, if they just won at this game. I would hope that they would find the grids on my body that felt only joy and pleasure, no shame, and I could save that code. But because I spent so much time nursing an awkwardness and hesitation with my body, even the few partners who were mindful of my pleasure over theirs (after theirs) would eventually give up and just stick to the game. The men I have dated have always been kind, or, at the very least, unmindful of what I saw to be glaring mistakes with my body.

If there has ever been any shame sent my way, for me, it has been outside of relationships. A friend whose eyes keep drifting to the hair on your face; a problematic student in your TA class whom you're standing over who looks pointedly at the discolouration on your chin, making it obvious they want you to know they have noticed; your cousin making a joke about you being a woolly mammoth; a close friend who dances around addressing acne on your face directly, by asking you about your current skincare; someone else telling you how hot you looked in a picture when you were 20 kg lighter. Like it was a drink sent my way in a bar by a stranger, the shame sent my way is intentioned to be wordless, to leave no traces. But I see it. Percolating like salt on their tongue. For so long I've downed that drink, assuming this shame comes natural to me. But shame is always outside of you. Shame is an arrow that quivers on a bow, held up by humans with white, salt-coated tongues.

One summer in Vancouver, somewhere in the middle of July, my friend Rachel invited me to join her and some friends for an afternoon at the clothing-optional beach in our university campus. That wasn't how it was worded, of course, just that all of us knew Wreck Beach was clothing-optional. No surprise that I optioned to keep my clothes on. But this memory isn't about my discomfort with nudity. It's about the revelation of my friends' acceptance of my decision. Until that point in time, I had, especially in India, been accustomed to a certain pressure to be explicitly sex-positive. Which I was, of course, but often felt at odds with having to discuss sexual acts and sex lives to prove how feminist we all were. And so I waited for someone to gently ask or suggest if I wasn't too hot, or if I had ever been to such a beach before, something, anything. But it never came up. My friends did their thing, and I did mine.

We sat there, a little off the entrance of the thin strip of rocky beach, eating blueberries and grapes, cold and bursting with summer. We read, chatted, swam, ate. After an hour I started feeling hot, and considered, for a moment, taking my clothes off. It would be the first time in my adult life that I would be out in public in anything but a baggy top. I thought of the vulgarities of excess and how, even in my head, there was something hyper-sexual about someone with big breasts, more-than-necessary breasts, even on a clothing-optional beach. Maybe in another ten minutes, I thought. I rolled my sleeves and leggings up as far back as they would go. Baby steps. Some more time passed and I was beginning to deeply regret the cotton-wool blend shirt and lycra leggings I was wearing to an afternoon on the beach (clothing was optional but dressing sense should have been mandatory). I fidgeted with the ends of my shirt, trying to not make it a big thing in my head. And then I saw a couple of men pass us on their way further down the beach. They looked young, most probably students at my university. They didn't look at us, so it's not like it was the fear of judgement that made me stop, but it immediately brought me out of the moment. I had almost believed for a second that this was it, all there was in the world, the four of us, the warm blue sea, a couple of seagulls and the coolness of the rock I was leaning on.

A few minutes later, another pair of men passed in front of us. Fellow Indians who did glance at us. I'm wont to reading any male gaze, especially in a clothing-optional beach as intrusive or sexual, but I suppose it would be best if I termed it a surveyor's gaze—a taking stock of one's surroundings. One of them looked at my friends for a quick second before meeting my eye. We immediately looked away, startled by this forced acknowledgement of kinship. Maybe I'm reading into something that doesn't exist, but I could sense it then. As if there was a moral code specific to the countries we've grown up in, minutely attuned to the colours of our skin. The two men continued on the beach; both parties remained fully clothed. The bow was pulled back, taut. I popped a blueberry in my mouth and pierced it between my front teeth so it exploded, cool and sour.

When we were younger, Varun and I were thrown into most classes together. Badminton, tennis, art, skating—we did it together, discovering our varied proficiencies. I want to say that Varun and I learnt swimming 'together', but that might be stretching the truth. It is true that we both started classes on the same day, but he took to it like a baby seal. The instructor would be prying my fingers off the tiled edges of the pool and talking to me about form, while Varun gently bobbed up and down in the deep end, chilling without a float. I was a little under five feet at the time, and the pool started off at four feet before getting consistently deeper until it was ten feet deep at the other end of the pool. I hated the sensation of losing my footing, so I'd stand terrified at the beginning of the pool. The only thing that kept me going in the classes, the only thing I nursed healthier than fear was pride. I would indeed rather have drowned than leave the pool because I was too scared. So I turned up for every class, and out of pride, learnt how to swim, and out of fear, did it quickly. Our instructor capitalized on my combination of ego and masochism by throwing me into swimming competitions held at the club. He knew I'd do well because I'd want to touch the deep end of the pool and come back as quickly as possible. Win-win. Somewhere in all of that, Varun also learnt to swim, but preferred to bob up and down like a cork in different corners of the pool.

I'd psyche myself into getting over my fear by following

Varun into the deep end, trying not to panic when my feet couldn't touch the ceramic floor of the pool any more. Varun would float ahead of me, tuned out completely from the world, and I'd try to take my time in the deep end, driving away thoughts of the drains in the pool violently sucking me in. I tried copying what Varun did—I really wanted to float, to feel as calm as he did. But I'd only end up becoming vertical if I was still in the waters. One day, as I struggled in the middle of the pool, a chunky brown foot floated in front of me. I rubbed the water out of my eyes, felt it burning through my nose and held on to the foot. I looked up at the human it was attached to—just my brother, floating around the pool, offering his foot to me as a life jacket. I turned to thank him and he looked at me, his face daring me to mention this at all. So I shut my mouth immediately, understanding that he'd do this only if I let him do it his way, which was for me to not make a big deal of it. Varun's leg always remained a constant.

In the summer of 2009, when a couple of my friends, Varun and I went white-water rafting in the Ganga, our rafting instructor politely asked all the heavier people in the raft to 'volunteer' to jump into the water. He wanted to demonstrate how to survive a raft overturning, but he could do it only with thinner people. Varun and my friend Shodhan immediately plopped into the river. I sat in my seat staring at the instructor for a hot second, trying to establish dominance, before sliding off the raft in resignation. We all had life jackets on, so I knew

I wouldn't drown. I floated on my back with my eyes closed for a couple of minutes—while the thin folks learnt vital survival skills—marvelling at how far I'd come from being fearful of water. Someone called out to me when I opened my eyes and flipped myself over, only to see that I had drifted much farther away from the raft. I panicked again, trying not to think of how strong river currents could be, trying not to cry. A majestic foot appeared next to me once more. Even then, there was always Varun, thoroughly exasperated with my childish fear, but always sparing me a foot.

In all my years of dealing with despair and panic, it is the promise of contact that comforts me. I dream of textures and sensations I know—Ammama's soft, papery palms, Nanna's cheekbones when I hold his face affectionately, Varun's tight, nearly unbreathable hugs, how heavy his arm feels on my shoulder when he's being affectionate, how small my mother's shoulders are measured through my embrace. I dream of textures and sensations I don't yet know, or have known once and forgotten. When I wake up in the middle of the night in panic, or after disordered sleep, I calm myself by imagining the weight of an arm on my waist cradling me to sleep. Just a little while longer, I tell myself, a little longer. At this point I don't know which question that is an answer to, but I know it's important for me to hear. After a particularly drunken experience with a quiet, kind boy I met in Vancouver, I cried for a whole day, finding it hard to get out of bed, not knowing why I was crying.

The physical intimacies of living with the people you love is what I deeply miss when living alone. I want to be held by someone. I want to hold someone. This longing isn't for romance, but intimacy. I still remember being four or five, my cousin lifting me up and placing me on her hip, me registering with surprise just how frail she felt as my legs wrapped around her bone, and I teetered against her body. I can feel friends balancing my weight and the bike's weight on their feet for a split second as I climb on. I'm sure it is physically improbable, but I can feel them brace their lower body for that split second when I heave myself on to the bike. I remember feeling this with uncles or aunts who picked me up and threw me up in the air to catch me, a squeal of shock and thrill, a moment of uncertainty before flesh rushed in to hold you and broke your fall.

It's always the promise of contact that brings me back to reality, assures me that this waking world is, in fact, real, even if, for the moment, slightly out of reach. Perhaps the only thing reminding me I am, in fact, here.

After that despondent weekend with the quiet, kind boy in Vancouver, when I finally made it out of bed to buy groceries to feed myself, I remember texting him—*I just realized it's the first time in a long time that I've been held.*

Death

The languages of grief are plenty and untranslatable. When Tatha, my paternal grandfather, died, it had already been a painful, long-drawn-out process. He had been ailing for a few years and hospitalized so frequently that it could have easily become part of our schedules. In his last hospitalization before death, Varun and I didn't visit him, assuming he would be back home. Maamma came over to us one evening and said that Tatha had declared that he would see us at home, there was no need to come to the hospital. Over the course of the month, when we realized he was probably not going to make it, I didn't want to visit, selfishly scared of what I'd see. Just the day before he was to be taken off life support and brought home, I visited him with Nanna in the ICU. It had taken a second to recognize the man on the bed, almost two feet smaller than my grandfather was, curled up like a baby, riven with tubes and needles. I stood next to him, unsure of anything except the heart-rate monitor that assured me he was still alive. Nanna came and said, 'Look at who's come! It's Shruti!', and Tatha's eyes slowly swept across to me, the briefest flicker of recognition. Looking into the eyes of someone I loved and not seeing recognition there really affected me. What was the point of living a full life when this was how it all ended? He passed away in his son's house, in his room, surrounded by his five children, as he drew his last breath. For days I would ask Nanna, 'Do you think he knew that I did come to see him? Did he know we were all there?'

Once our relatives had left and it was just the five of us again at home, I offered to move in to Maamma's and Tatha's room. I didn't want Maamma to feel alone. It had been difficult for them to make the move from Hyderabad to our home in Gurgaon anyway, uprooting their entire lives to live with us because Tatha wasn't keeping well and they would have more support here. The first night after everyone left, I went into Maamma's room with my blanket. 'Maamma, don't worry, I'll be your new roommate now!' I joked, and she chuckled. That night, when I tossed in bed, Maamma mumbled immediately, 'Do you want me to massage your feet?' Towards the end of his days, Tatha would find it hard to sleep, his legs twitching and jerking involuntarily all night. We'd often find the light on in their room late into the night, Maamma massaging his feet. I paused awkwardly. She had thought I was Tatha. 'Maamma…it's me, Shruti…' Some more silence, perhaps my voice summoning her back into this reality. 'Oh, yes, yes, I know.' Maamma and I would spend a lot of time talking about

Tatha, and when we didn't, she would listen to audio cassettes of him in his vocal classes over and over until the Walkman's batteries drained out. I'd often wake up to her crying under the thick winter duvets, possibly keeping it down because I was around and she didn't want to make me sad. One day, she removed Tatha's picture from the wall and put it inside her cupboard. 'I know you're finding it difficult to see his face like that, so I kept it inside.' I told her it was completely okay, that it was her room, she got to decide. Maamma shook her head. 'I don't need a picture to remind me of him. And all I need to do is open the cupboard to see him.' We spoke about how restful Tatha looked when he finally passed, how beautiful it was that everyone was around him, and that we played his favourite song by Balamuralikrishna on a loop. She told me it was a blessing to pass like that. I asked her if there was a song she would like played when she passed, and she thought about it for a second and chose another song by Balamuralikrishna. Even in grief, Maamma's reflex was to make everyone around her happy. I keep thinking how presumptuous it was of me to decide to move in without checking if that's what she wanted. Maybe she didn't want anyone in that space, maybe she wanted a moment to herself, to register the absence of Tatha in the room that still smelt of Brut, Old Spice and Bajaj almond oil. I thought I was comforting her by moving in, but who was doing whom the favour? The days didn't last too long. In the two years between Tatha's death and Maamma's, she would spend half the year with my uncles abroad. Then I moved to Pune in July 2011 and she slipped on the stairs and fell to her death that October. I wasn't there for her funeral, it was the only time Nanna had gently suggested we didn't. 'She doesn't look like herself,' he said, 'it's not how you remember her.' I made sure they played her song.

They say a life filled with love necessarily involves a life filled with the fear of that love's loss. All through my childhood, irrespective of whether I felt close to Amma or not, I'd formed a habit of seeking her out first thing when I woke up in the morning. I'd open my eyes, and fumble in the darkness of early dawn for a bit before gliding slowly through the house and making my way—like a bat using echolocation—to the sounds from whichever room that indicated that Amma was there. Most times, she'd be in the kitchen, hurrying to pack our lunches. I'd stand in the kitchen doorway, not saying a word (both of us need time to fully wake up and be social), with all the world's patience for the moment that Amma would turn around and look at me. Sometimes, she'd smile and ask me a question. Sometimes she'd look up for a second to wish me a good morning. Perhaps on rare days she wouldn't say anything at all, finish whatever was urgent and look at me and offer a pat on the head. It didn't matter, though, my heart was always full because my mother was alive, and she was there. I could now get on with my day. I noticed the remnants of that habit even through the years of living alone—I'd wake up and, for a brief moment, before I even fully opened my eyes, seek out the lilting music of utensils in the kitchen before I'd remember she was not here.

The threat of loss.

Things you cannot say to your mother when she is fighting for her life in the hospital: I'm not scared that you're dying. I've *always been* scared. I've grown up mourning your impending death. I brace for the moment when the only permanence in my life is taken away, so when the threat of it actually looms, I have already made my peace with it. Is making your peace with something the same as wishing for it? I don't wish for you to be in pain. I don't like visiting you in the ICU during visiting hours, because there are always other people around and I can't talk to you in the way that I really want to. I fear I will explode into tears if you talk to me for too long, so I'm going to busy myself with functional things instead and reassure you that everything at home is being well managed. I would rather go to work every day and pretend that this is just another routine, my edits on a page, my mother on a ventilator. I want to talk to you about death, about your death, about Nanna's death, about why you won't let anyone comfort you when you're grieving, tell me about how I can comfort you when you're grieving. Is this all the loneliness and sadness you've folded away from when Tatha was sick and passed away, from when Maamma was depressed and she passed away, from when Varun and I left home and suddenly everything in our house was just an echo? Tell me about what you're thinking of right now. Do you remember when the anaesthesia started kicking in and you reached out, motioning vaguely for someone, and I walked up to hold your hand? Do you remember pulling your hand away, indicating that it was Nanna you were asking for? I want you to know I wasn't hurt, but it reminded me that I don't have the right language to comfort you, even though you've always known mine. What if I asked Nanna, would he tell me how to be that person that everyone wanted when they were scared?

Nanna waited for me at the entrance to the hospital today, when I came in from work, and I knew something had happened to you. He put an arm around me and said, 'Don't panic, but Amma has been moved to the ICU. She'll be fine.' I didn't panic. I briefly considered our lives without you, but that was all. Will I grow into your body as I grow older? Are you and I bound by the same failings of our flesh? We were told to wait for a night or two, see if you'd make it out alive. Fifty-four is still quite young, Nanna and the doctors said, so you should pull through. Your father was fifty-six when he passed away. Did you wonder if you and your father shared the same codings of the flesh? I can't seem to cry or feel sad about anything, not even the thought that tomorrow you might not be alive. Instead, I am productive, and angry. I go to work every day, update everyone who checks in, but I am so angry. I want to remind you of all the hurtful things you've said to me and have you tell me all the words I have hurt you with, because none of them will have mattered. Why did we say them if it was going to come down to this, the threat of you leaving? When you're better, when we all come back from this, will you talk to me about things? When you come back, everything will change. Will you write down some things for me, some kind of hex I can chant for the times when you will not be around? Are you scared when visiting hours end and there's no one around for you to talk to? Do you keep time with your pulse beeping on the machine? Will you find a way of holding me even after you're gone? Do I make you proud?

Things you should say to her but don't: I love you. Come back home. Let me hold you.

In 2017, we lost our friend Mrunmayi unexpectedly at the age of twenty-six to dengue. The last memory I have of her is under the streetlight of her house tucked away in a quiet corner of Pune, hugging her. I was with Shweta—the three of us close, but her and Mrunmayi inseparable. Moon—we all called her—lost her father three weeks before she passed away, both huge, incomparable losses. Her shoulder blades, so hollow and frail, like a bird's, trembling away under my palms as we said goodbye and left her to process this. The last thing

I remember is looking up at her room and, after a second, watching the lights go off. Even through her grief, the last thing she asked me was about some update from my work (which had brought me to Pune). Typical Moonie, to always make space for you and remember, no matter what she was going through. There are so many ways I can look at this—that I could be there when her father passed away, that I could immediately be there when she passed away. Losing someone so bright, this young, and this unfairly shook something inside all of us. How does life begin to ration out such pain and how is a human being supposed to endure this?

With Moon's passing, there is a rage that nothing has changed and life has simply gone on, and a dread that, in fact, everything had. If I were to suddenly disappear, I realized, perhaps no one would notice immediately. There's not one person with whom I talk to every day, who would immediately sense something wrong if I didn't at least get in touch once during the day. Her death was a flare in the night sky, revealing to all of us our own place on the map. Moonie's passing meant that I could suddenly see where I stood. Where did I stand? What can I say I have in all my years of living?

There is a hubris to thinking of your own death. The sheer force of one's complexity as a human being with desires and thoughts and wants somehow means more than the others, and therefore it will be you who will stick around, see others leave. But Moon's passing changed everything for me. How

I thought about sickness, how I approached my friendships thereon, what I wanted to focus on in this short, short life. Perhaps the biggest fear of living alone and single is that you haven't made an impact in anyone else's life because they're all self-sustained units. As much as my parents love me, they always have each other first. A lot of my best friends are married or have partners. Who could I say was my person? What would I be leaving behind when I died? It'll be two years to her passing soon, and some days I reel under the delayed shock. A shared memory pops up on Facebook, or an old chat in a Gmail search, a memory of us cackling over something. She lives on digitally, and I can't ever be sure this is the kinder thing. Shweta and I talk about her and to her endlessly, as if she were around, reading our group texts and intending to respond as soon as she got a moment to herself. But grief is delicate and knotty. Sometimes remembering is too much, and sometimes not remembering is treason. We suss each other's grief every day, navigating our loss, keeping each other in our line of sight, crying, laughing. On some days, it hits me like a brick that she's not here, how time has just passed and how I seem to be functioning as if nothing has happened. Everything feels light and unreal, until I remember her firmly planting her feet on each side of a scooter heavier than her, and waiting—as I, for a second, unsteered, weightless, hurtling towards every uncertainty—to steady us both.

I wonder if the methods of our individual grieving are

inherent in us, or derived from behaviours we learn from those around us. At home, all of us grieve matter-of-factly. Nanna is approachable and stoic, Amma is inaccessible but functional, Varun just internalizes everything until it becomes a fact of life, a piece of data. From them I've learnt that irrespective of how painful the fact is, people are there one day, and then they aren't. And since this has overlapped with how I grew up—friends were there one day and then they weren't—I seemed to have accepted the finality of both. It's not that I don't understand the difference between death and distance, but that their effects on my life are similar, both huge dislocations that I have to absorb by spreading them across into spider-like tremors of various anxieties in my daily life.

Amma always has this one story from when I was a toddler that typifies how given I was to the dramatic. If something upset me, I would waddle out of the room, huffing my disapproval—which I'm sure was a sight, considering I was bald and possibly only in a nappy or a diaper. A minute or two would pass, and if no one followed me, I would make another appearance, saying, 'Hello? Can someone turn the light on in that room please? I'm crying.' I obviously don't remember this, but it sounds exactly like something I would do. Whenever Amma repeats this story, I am reminded of another one, one from my own memory. I must have been about nine or ten when something Amma said upset or hurt me. I stormed into my bathroom (because I shared a room with Varun for most of our life together), bawling. The bucket poised under the tap was empty and an idea struck me. I would cry into the bucket, fill it up with my tears and then show Amma how much she had hurt me. And so I cried—I rested my hands on my wobbly knees, bending over the bucket and milking every tear out for what seemed like hours. The anger or hurt subsided long before determination set in. It couldn't be that hard. So I invoked previous grievances, lashing myself with the memories of earlier injustices until I was absolutely spent. I squeezed my eyes shut so forcefully I'm sure a few more tears would've fallen out due to the sheer impact. I opened my eyes, confident that I had at least filled it halfway. My tears barely covered the base of the bucket. It looked, at best, as if the tap had leaked for a second or two after being shut off. I learnt my humility tables that day. I learnt two things that day that will suffice me for this lifetime. One: Either I was not as hurt as I thought, or that the amount of tears are (sometimes) no proof of your hurt. Two: I am really, really bad at approximating anything.

It's a funny story, but it also said something about how early on in life I had somehow caught the pulse of something—that grief can also exist outside of us and need witnessing for true relief or release.

You can't have chronic illness and not think of your own death. I'm already at high risk of ovarian and uterine cancers, heart disease and irregularities, diabetes, thyroid inflammation, mental illness, obesity and metabolic disorders. Add to it potential connections between the oral contraceptive pill and mood disorders, breast cancer, anxiety and deteriorating mental health. I joke that it's either the syndrome or the treatment that will eventually be the death of me. Any new pain I register sets off the most severe alarm and I catch myself quickly wondering if this is how I'll go, if this is what will be the end of me. Without an overarching passion, like Beth, I'm always living on borrowed time. I am often reminded of a joke that goes something like, 'I don't trust women. You shouldn't trust anything that bleeds for five days and still doesn't die.' On the fifteenth, thirtieth and forty-fifth day of bleeding, I crumble in a heap in the bathroom, bawling. This is impossible, I am not human. Nothing is supposed to live like this and go on like this. I grieve for a body that I don't have in this life. I grieve for the one that I do.

2011–2013 passed me by in a blur. My chronic illness flared up full blast; I had broken up what would be the longest relationship of my life; and I had quit my job in journalism, unsure of what to do next. I came back to Delhi and found a job in a publishing house there, trying to nurse my heart and body back to health. Within three months of my moving back, Amma would be hospitalized again, and we would almost lose her. At the age of twenty-four, with the loss of the body, the loss of love and the threat of loss of a loved one, something nefarious seemed to click together after years of tinkering. A catapult stretching relentlessly and painfully over the years before it snapped into a furious kinetic energy that shot me so deep out into the stratosphere that I found myself wholly unanchored for the first time, with no way of knowing which way was up and which way was down.

II
Weightlessness

rudderless / free / dissolving / flowing
being let go
letting go

Introduction

2018.

There's a room in a house that I haven't yet seen, that has been marked for me. I find it typical of the life I lead. On a phone call, Amma tells me she's planning to put up a collage of my baby pictures in the room, to officially christen it. Through this two-week process of moving homes and cities, the idea of me floats around like a spirit summoned from a parallel universe to be a crucial part of my family's decisions.

I wake up every day to a steady trickling in of calls, and text messages on our family group chat. 'Which of the two rooms would you like?' my father asks me one day, on a phone call he makes at 6 a.m. He knows I'm never awake then. Regardless, he goes on to describe the facets of each room in precise detail. 'The first room overlooks the community park but it gets hot earlier in the day. The second room overlooks the huge garbage dump outside the complex, but you can see the sunset...when it's not smoggy,' he calculates. Choices,

choices. I tell him I'll be happy with either, it really doesn't make that much of a difference.

'Nanna was hoping he could use one room as a study... once you've chosen your room, of course...' Amma trails off another morning. A younger me would have been exasperated eventually at this charade, but I am now trained to read their acts of fondness and love. This is their language, they speak it differently. And yet, I want to scream into the phone, 'How does it matter, Amma! I'm 2,000 km away, I don't even live there!'

This is a strange way of existing—as a ghost in everyone's life. I don't actually take up any physical space, but my absence has a form, a shape, a clear outline that is always at hand. There's a space that's demarcated for me when I visit family and friends and, yet, by necessity, it is something that can be replaced quickly. The first time I realized this was when I was thirteen, and had just moved from Mumbai to Delhi. This was the first time I registered the weight of leaving because I was old enough to do the delicate mathematics involving leaving and loss. Over that summer in Mumbai, my friends and I made many determined, tearful promises to meet again. Our parents couldn't ruin our friendship. No, I would use up every vacation to come back if I had to. And in between those vacations, we would drown each other in snail mail. We held hands that summer, sure that nothing could come between us.

Then, as the months went by, each of those promises tapered off. The newness of everything in a new school was more consuming than I had anticipated, and I suppose the routineness of everything for my friends back in Mumbai was too. At sixteen, when I had the chance to visit Mumbai for a weekend, I immediately called up each of my friends in Mumbai to make plans, but only two were available to meet (separately).

I don't remember what those brief meetings were like now. There were hugs and idle gossip, and a lot of shy wonder at how much the other had changed. Some exclamations at the new language that had crept into my system ('You say *arre* now', 'You Delhi people say *oi* a lot'), and some attempts at rekindling the old connection by invoking the names of old crushes. But the inner texture of that evening was entirely closed off to me. Did I feel a sense of homecoming? My old circuitry alive again, here with the people I loved in the spaces that I had loved them in. Or did I now feel disoriented being in those spaces, which had seemed so much more expansive in my memories? 'Has our school always been this small and cramped?' I remember asking my friend. 'Don't know…this is how it's always been,' she said, disinterested in the stupidity of my question. We walked around school for a bit in silence, unsure of what to say. I remember her telling me about her new classroom best friend, which she assured me was different from her 'all time' best friend, which I still was. I remember wondering if I had disappointed her.

Slightly thrown off by this information, I think I rattled

off all the names of people from her life that I had made a point to remember, so eager to prove that I had, in fact, not changed at all. Years later, I would sign up for the TOEFL exam to prove my mastery over the English language for my studies abroad, and would notice that the fine print mentioned that these results would be valid only for two years. The only relationship someone from the global south could have with English, apparently, is one of evaporation. Like a bottle of nail-polish remover, you've got to keep the cap tightened with English, or it'll sublimate off your tongue. Perhaps it's not too different with friendship either, because there I was, in Mumbai, sitting with my friend on a parapet inside our school premises, trying to prove my continued proficiency in friendship.

'How are Uncle and Aunty? And your brother? Oh, what about that cousin of yours who you had a fight with in sixth standard? Is your room still purple?'

'Wait, you actually remember that?' my friend asked, part incredulous, part impressed, and it suddenly seemed like everything would go back to how it was. Despite what anyone said, maybe I could keep my friends forever. All it took was being a good remember-er. She perked up immediately, perhaps validated that I wasn't fully a lost cause. As we walked towards her building (which I made a point of demonstrating that I still remembered the route to by walking a step ahead of her), she tried returning the favour by asking about my family.

'And how are your parents? And...sorry, what was your brother's name again?'

'Who? Varun?' I asked.

'Oh, yeah! Sorry, sorry, Varun.'

How gloriously our hubrises come crashing. How many hours had the three of us spent together, my brother, my friend and I, after school, before school, on holidays, marinating in kiddie pools in summer? Perhaps it was natural to forget, but that minor erasure stayed with me, and I learnt a difficult but important lesson in humility. How else do you explain the grandeur and delusion in assuming that people will be unable to carry on without you? That you're the piece that will glue everything back together, if only you could be there. But not only was I not there, my friend seemed to have carried on perfectly without me, minor details of my life fading out of her memory as new ones with new friends made their way in.

After that initial heartbreak, the subsequent moves became easier. I knew no matter how much we proclaimed we'd be in touch forever and nothing would change, everything kind of would. I still continued remembering most things from my friends' lives, huge and tiny. My memory seemed to work independently of any outcome, because no amount of remembering could bring back old friends or transport you to an old life. It was like an over-industrious, inefficient team that I didn't have the heart to lay off, so I didn't put up a fight against this forced archival. At sixteen, I realized that because you're the one who leaves, you're almost always the one who remembers.

By the time I'm in my early twenties, home ends up on the list of places I don't really belong to either. By the time I'm twenty-eight and visit my family during a break in my postgrad semester, I write in one of my journal entries: *The me-shaped hole is now a me-shaped spectre that takes up no physical space and dimension in my loved ones' lives.*

Over the second half of my twenties, my friend Suraj and I come up with a phrase we overuse everywhere: 'Oh pfft, we don't even live here.' It applies to everything. 'Well, I mean I don't even live here,' Suraj will text me after destroying an airport bathroom after a particularly spicy meal, more for himself than for anyone else. In a crowded elevator, Suraj will hurriedly ask, 'Please tell me this restaurant has decent *facilities…*', and our friend immediately says, 'Oh, this place has really good toilets, can you hold it in until we get there?' A snigger passes around in the elevator. Suraj will mumble, 'Whatever…I don't even live here!', and scurry out of the elevator just as the doors open.

We're aware of how faulty this logic is. As if embarrassment can only stick to people who stick around. We use it like a hex to ward off the actual anxiety of not feeling we belong to any one place in particular, a lightweight phrase that somehow valiantly carries the unbearable weight of displacement.

I've often wondered if we were on to something bigger when we first came up with the phrase, a sort of accidental truth-making. Given the temporariness of each place I've lived in, I'm at a loss when asks where I'm from. Because I moved around so much as a child, and continued that of my own volition as an adult, I don't really know where home is on a map. The only identities I've had have been delayed ones. So, when I moved from Delhi to Mumbai, I was the kid from Delhi. But in Delhi I was the kid from Bengaluru, and so on.

'*For the moment* I'm in Chennai,' I'd say, finishing off the sentence in my head, 'but I wouldn't say I *live* there.' As if it were the most crucial misreading of me, to believe that I lived in a city, or belonged to one. If you took a map and pinned each city I've lived in, I'd exist somewhere in the tautness of the string attaching one point to the other.

Of course, I don't tell Amma any of that when she brings up the room again. In a few weeks, I know the commotion will die down and whenever it is that I visit this new house, I'll slip into whichever room has the framed collage of me up. Once I understand my place in the order, it's a light living. *I don't even live here.*

'So where are you really from?' I'm asked now and then, and I can only apologetically offer a list of places I've passed through. In that litany, I cross my fingers and hope that people will understand that I'm a messy agglutinate of all the places I've ever lived in. Like a hologram created by splitting up light beams, a permanent record of all the places I've lived, reflected off me.

And as with all things that are required to fit into the tiniest dimensions for efficient and optimal portability, I require assembly.

Travel

This is how I unpack myself in a new city—a pattern that has unveiled itself in retrospect. There always has to be a base route to begin. In Vancouver, it is the one from my place to the nearest grocery store, ten blocks away. It's a straight line, and one I'll use the most. The first time we go there is with my uncle, aunt, Sharat and Priya, who graciously make the trek with me from Maryland in the US to Vancouver in Canada, to settle me in. There's a beautiful, tacit understanding that they'll help cushion the inevitable assault on my cultural senses, as someone who's never been out of the country. And yet, I write in my journal, 'The West just feels like any big city in India except with more "foreigners"', and, a little while later, 'upper-middle-class aesthetics look the same everywhere'. But back to my unpacking: I follow this base route over and over, until it feels comfortable, until it feels like my route, something I can traverse with my eyes closed. On the base route, I am no longer a stranger to this country. In those ten blocks, I could be anyone, perhaps I could even have been born there. Once the gelatinous beginnings of belonging set, I start venturing out on other routes—which always either end, begin or pass through the base route at some point. Home to university, university to grocery store, home to the movieplex downtown. Grid by grid, I settle into the city. Often, it has taken an entire year by the time I have registered I am in a new place, I have unpacked and settled. In Vancouver, it takes me a little over a year and a half to feel comfortable with the cityscape. As my unmooring grows over the years, I hold on to these patterns even more strongly—like a mountaineer, I lead the climb and set up my ropes. I abseil to control my descent into an alien land.

There was always a difference between moving and travelling to me, even as a child. Both were exciting, but one was a lot more enjoyable than the other because it wasn't permanent. My life tended so much to the former that it affected my desire (or lack of) for the latter. As a family we'd go on short vacations, of course, but it was devoid of any romanticization for me. It was thrilling to be somewhere new but it was always the journey that I loved. The smell of train stations, the bleary-eyed crack-of-dawn wake-up calls, the busy shuffling of feet before everyone crammed into a car or a van. There were always snacks along the way, potato wafers, cream biscuits, chilli chicken, cutlets tasting a little like the moist foil they were heated in. I loved it all. By the time I was old enough to go on trips with friends, the joy of travel for me was the joy of getting away with the people I loved. And once I started travelling for work, my brain seemed to confer that there was little difference between travelling, visiting and living in a place. Aren't all three eventually just the same question of belonging? *How do you fit in here?* And so I end up approaching travel like I have grown up approaching geographic dislocation, inside out.

As a result, I rough up against what, to me, is the over-romanticization of travel in our generation, this pressure of stepping out as the only valuable method of exploring a new city. I say this with envy, or jealousy, because it doesn't come naturally to me, and I've felt so lonely in this aberration that I wish it did. Instead, I end up wanting to experience what the city feels like *on the inside* first. What can I buy from the convenience store down the road, what plays on local cable, what do targeted ads look like on my phone in this city? This isn't to say that I will refuse to step out of my accommodation, but just that if left to myself, my travel itinerary would be wholly disappointing to someone else. So when I travel with friends, especially extroverts who get bored easily, I let them make the plans and we reach a tacit understanding, where I join them in the plans I feel I am up to.

What is it that we seek when we travel to a new city? Is it the rush of heading into an unknown experience? Is it the physical validation of having researched that experience for months first? Is it the joy of learning things around you and about you? How important is it, in each of these factors, that you be the first to do so? Can there really be an authentic tourist experience of a city? I'm always slightly amused and puzzled when someone insists on doing 'off the beaten path' things in a city, only to google these things off a list, accessible to anyone else with an Internet connection and the same exact question. I find an odd comfort in guided tours and visiting overcrowded touristy places, and I suspect this is because, for once, I am represented accurately, as an outsider. My existence in that moment—in that bar where I might stick out like a sore thumb and make myself conspicuous, while fumbling with new currency notes in front of a cashier, in quickly picking up on which side of the escalator I should stand on—is of cathartic equilibrium. My movements might sporadically reveal or disguise the fact that I've been transplanted there: I am not a local, and don't need to attempt to parade as one. There is a giddiness in this syncing, this calibration. I wave the flag, proud and relieved, 'Not from Here!'

My attachment to a place is always delayed because I don't think I've ever been truly present in a city when I'm living there. This is both literal and metaphorical. All my identity cards have an address that I don't live at any more, my electoral card and bank accounts always one city behind in updation.

But also that when I move, it takes a while to unpack my suitcase, my belongings, myself, and for the world to stop spinning. And then, only then, do I get to fill out an exit form for the city I just left, file my claims, and, in the safety of the miles between that city and this, encash my experiences into meaning and memories. The feeling of belonging, or having belonged to, is a reimbursement. You can access it only once you've finished the ride. More often than not, the people I love, my family, old friends and, every now and then, a romantic partner will be miles away, and I end up, even in a new city, with the circadian rhythms of my loved ones from at least three time zones away. Unsurprisingly, I find it easier, and more rewarding, to attach sentiment to objects instead—and if this were a book read in a first-year English-literature class, someone would scribble on the margin 'but of course!'.

A soap I used (only) in Delhi will always remind me of the cold marble flooring in my bathroom, my feet absently running back and forth over a large crack beneath the sink. I've sneakily borrowed my grandfather's phone to text some boy in class, and I prop my upper body on the sink while I wait for the bucket of water to fill up. I can always smell dinner by this point. Delhi is always the nip in the air in November, the air heavy with the smoke of crackers, musky and percolating into microscopic nodules in your throat. It's always evening, the ground already turning a little uncomfortable, forcing you to quicken your steps. It is your first hot-water bath of the season, and the crinkling of winter clothes when taken out of a long summer hibernation spent marinating in mothballs. Pune is amusingly weatherless—just perfect, not too cool or hot or humid—and somehow the promise of an endless night. When I lived there, my friends got off work after closing the next day's newspaper edition, so the city came alive with possibility only after that. The streets are always buzzing with people, and they're always a lot younger than you. Mumbai is the smell of salt in the air and fish, black clouds in the afternoon, and the particular damp-with-sweat smell of Fiat taxis with their hot metal handles, towel-seating worn thin by countless passengers, everyone's faces in a traffic jam blinking red, yellow, red, yellow, red, yellow. Chennai is early mornings, street dogs, packets of curd and a violent, aggressive, hostile heat, the likes of which I have not encountered before. It is a city I struggle to call home but feel a fondness the second I step outside it. And yet, to each city, one thing is common. I remember each of them in the rains. Their specificities suspended for the length of the shower. Heat, dust, humidity, mist, smog, aggression, exhaustion, ennui. The rain resets it all, a palate cleanser.

As far as I can remember, I've always been an unsettled flyer. Perhaps it is only because of exposure therapy, and the fact that there is so much data to corroborate that flying is the safest form of transport that I've managed to sit through each flight. The course at UBC (University of British Columbia) in Vancouver was one I had had my eye on for a while. But the thought of sitting in long-haul flights alone, with no escape from my thoughts, gave me a lot of anxiety, and I let the idea be. But, in 2015, when I somehow made the anxious journey to the US (on my way to Canada), on two back-to-back long-hauls, I landed in Washington DC as a new person. I had conquered one of my biggest fears; I didn't know what I'd done to overcome it, but somehow I had done it. 'I've no jet lag at all!' I gushed into my first Skype call with my family back in India.

On our way to Vancouver, my cousins and I flew to Seattle. It was the first time any of us was there, so the Boeing factory was at the top of our list. There I learnt that one of the airplane models I flew on, the Boeing 787, used carbon fibre on top of the aluminium scaffolding. Because these materials were so light, Boeing could now change the internal cabin pressure on flights from the equivalent of 8,000 feet altitude to 6,000 feet. Apparently, that meant lesser dehydration, more oxygen and, magically, less jet lag. The carbon fibre also allowed for bigger windows, enabling someone sitting in the centre aisle seats to still see the horizon. The tour guide explained that whenever people were fearful or uncomfortable with flying, it was mostly because they could not see the horizon unless they were all up in the window seat. With this new modification, you could always see the horizon—whether water to sky, or land to sky. I jotted all this down as the guide took us through the huge factory. But it was only later, on our car ride back, that I realized what had just happened. It's staggeringly humbling to find out, halfway across the world, on what I thought would be a boring trip to a Boeing factory, that what I took to be admirable personal growth and the overcoming of fear was, in fact, the silent humming of aeronautical engineering making incredible strides.

Inspirational aeronautics aside, something does change for me over the years. I make peace with my mortality. Years later, in 2018, as I fly back to Chennai from a work trip in Taiwan, our plane shakes and jitters over the South China Sea and then the Bay of Bengal. I manage to pass in and out of sleep, waking up only to think to myself that if this plane were to crash, to 'just make it quick'. The upkeep for fearing for your life is, every now and then, just too much to hold together.

Who do you text when you've landed? My parents will worry themselves sick and constantly remind me to share cab details with them when I'm travelling late at night. I groan inwardly every time I'm asked—I don't want my phone to be ringing while it's deep in my pocket and I'm in the middle of lugging heavy bags up three flights of stairs. But when I do, they're fast asleep, responding only the next day. As I land from Bangkok in Chennai, and am texting one of my closest friends, Shweta, who stands guard against the fortress of the paper-thin beauty of the late hours of night, always around, a force shield between me and the world, I think to myself—perhaps home is this feeling of relief. Who or what do we come home to?

Before I even begin to answer that giant of a question, a smaller but prouder one appears in front of it, blocking my way, fists on its hip, chest puffed out. 'Which home?' I clear my throat to recite the statement I've prepared over the years. 'Well, technically, I was born in...' I start but it shakes its head firmly—no, no, no. 'When you long for home, what is the physical place you imagine?' I fumble and pause. Where is home, indeed? Beyond the poetics of feeling and association, what physical dimensions does home occupy? If someone handed me a piece of paper and some crayons and asked me to draw my house, which one would I draw?

The longest I've ever lived in a house is thirteen years, in a cozy ground-floor townhouse in Gurgaon, the house my parents invested in and bought. Nineteen years our name was on the house papers, but for the last few we had rented it out because we didn't live in Delhi any more. When my family moved from Delhi to Mumbai in 2014, I didn't get to say a proper goodbye to the house—I was visiting my grandmother in Hyderabad when everyone else made the move. It affected me then too, but I knew better than to make a big deal of it, even to myself. It's our house, I told myself, we'll come back to it one day. I moved to Vancouver from Mumbai and then to Chennai. By the time I came back to Delhi, it was 2019. By the beginning of 2019, we had sold the house.

It's not until the last remaining anchor I had to a place on this planet disappeared that I realized something important about all the houses I've lived in, especially the Gurgaon house: I trust the houses that I live(d) in to hold parts of my psyche up that I cannot, I trust the brick and mortar to ease parts of my living. This realization, after fourteen years of living in the small, twice-owned house, which was always threatening decay and crumble. We drive by it one weekend, and I'm suddenly fifteen again, the same people, sitting in the same spots in the car, back in the corner of my world. Except, of course, most of the surrounding commercial establishment has changed. Everything looks so much narrower and congested, so alien, no longer mine. In the fourteen years I spent here, the neighbourhood (and city) grew with me. I watched as it grew from a civilizational hinterland to a sprawling, swan-like, corporate nightmare, and it watched me grow up and away. As we turn the corner to the lane our house is on, my throat catches. I haven't seen it for five years. Will it recognize me? I take a deep breath and look outside the window. There it is, the house that saw me grow. Smaller and more unassuming than I remember it. A fresh coat of paint (a homely, amiable beige) and a small square on the front door, blacker than the rest where our nameplate had once been hammered in. Even in the five seconds it may have taken to pass the house, I keep waiting for it to somehow (magically and impossibly) recognize me, give me a sign it still remembers me from the days where I sat in the small front garden with a book (and later, my phone), my feet up the chalky parapet, or all the times that I stuck half my body out of a chute next to the common bathroom, fiddling with the pressure valve to temper the aggressive but sputtering water pressure in our taps, massaging and cajoling the defunct innards, easing the old-age pains of this house with its permanent smell of damp concrete and pigeons. Even if the house recognizes me, it doesn't let on. 'And thaaaat was our house,' Nanna says definitively, as if there can be no closure without that express stating of things. As we turn away from it, I look back one last time, neck straining, soaking in snippets of the black iron grill that used to box the backyard from both monkeys and men. But the only house that was ever mine is already dusting its clothes off, preparing to welcome another family, looking through me, looking ahead.

The next few weekends are spent in emptying the storeroom of the house before the new owners move in. There's not much left, except for picture albums that won't survive another move, old books you can't move without an explosion of mould and fungus, journals and notebooks and class notes. The new owners are lovely, and ask us not to bother making the city-wide trek to Gurgaon every time. They offer to pack our things for us, calling us every now and then for guidance. Slowly, boxes start washing up in our new rented space, and I go through them one by one after nearly a decade. I'm still shaky from the anxiety episode in December, which ended in me moving back to Delhi, so it is at an opportune time that these messages in a bottle reach my shore. In a weird way, my old house finds a way to hold me up, one last time.

What did our lives come across as to the new owners? Was anything intimate or embarrassingly private revealed in our absence when they started moving in? Could they tell if we were sentimental or not? I'm always fascinated when I go house-hunting. How do other people live? If they're not around when you come by, what do their things say about them? What do my things say about me? If you picked apart my suitcase, heavy on medicines (99 per cent for stomach-related ailments) and books, low on clothes and footwear, what would you make of me? If someone had to walk into my room without me there, who would they conjure up in their mind's eye? Do I come across as someone who has it all together? I always think of the things I leave behind and what they say about me to the person who might walk in after me. Do the things we leave behind have a way of revealing, to absolute strangers, which direction we are headed?

I learnt recently that the human body takes orientation for granted. Impossible as it sounds, apparently it is actually quite easy to lose direction while flying, drowning or if you're stuck in an avalanche. For someone who has depended entirely on learning directions immediately in a new place, the idea is paralysing. Who would I be if not for my sense of direction? Where is the map that tells you if you're heading towards meaning or not? I read Internet theorists on an aviation forum, dissecting a recent Lion Air plane crash over Indonesia. Some argue that the crash into the Indian Ocean might have been because of compromised orientation. With crucial parts malfunctioning, the pilot could have mistaken down for up, plummeting into the ocean while assuming the plane was in ascent. In pitch-black darkness, with the moon reflecting off the water, it is easy to mistake the sea for the sky, a member notes. If you are ever stuck in an avalanche, someone else chimes in, it is recommended that you pee or spit and notice which direction the fluid falls in, and to crawl your way out in the opposite direction. How hard can it be? I think to myself in panic. Aren't our survival instincts inbuilt? It should be painfully obvious which way is out, right?

And yet.

Loneliness

Two things I love the most: making plans and then postponing them.

As an introvert, I usually plan social meetings outside my house, or at someone else's, two ways—as far off in the calendar from today as I can and, if possible, by clubbing them all together. Growing up with schools and colleges really far away (transit was always over an hour) meant it had to become an all-or-nothing scenario. You either turned up at college and attended every class, or you didn't make that trek. So now I usually end up with a day in the week where I'm moving from one plan to another, with no rest in between. Eventually, they all pile up for the one day and suddenly the stakes are too high. One of those plans moves, cancels or extends, and everything topples over.

You'd think I'd stop the pattern and learn to sprinkle my plans evenly through the week, but that holds another, bigger obstacle. In my anxiety-ridden universe, time works differently. If there's a day full of solitude ahead of me, except for that one meeting, I can't seem to relax until the meeting is done. I could have a good chunk of time before I'm to meet someone but somehow that land is arid, inhospitable. No other activity can grow there, I can't start anything new. I can sit down and read a book, do some chores or write, but my brain refuses—'You're leaving in three hours, it's too close a call.' So I'll scroll endlessly on my phone and eventually end up earlier to the meeting, because there seems to be nothing else I can actually do. This is why I'm envious of folks who utilize the immense pockets of time that seem out of my reach. My friend and housemate in Vancouver, Idalia, would wait until the absolute last second to catch the bus to UBC, calculating her trotting/jogging speed beforehand to make it to the bus. To me, the stakes were simply too high. I either made it to class well before time, or made my peace with missing it altogether.

I'm always preparing, expecting to be thrown off track.

Early 2018.

My father sits across from me on the sofa, the phone screen reflecting in his glasses as he books a cab for the airport. We've sat in strained silence the whole day, the one day he's in town visiting me. This one's on me, though. My father, like my mother and brother, is an easy presence, and will fit into the tiniest corners of anyone's life. I like to think I've got that from him, this contentment with whatever space is assigned to me in someone's life. It's me. As usual, something's wrong and I can't place it.

The night before, as we sat marinating in our own sweat, this Chennai wet hug, he asked me to turn the air conditioner on.

'Uhh, it kind of has been on for the last half-hour. Can't you hear it?'

My father looks baffled.

'I thought that was a water tanker...'

'That's the AC'.

'You really need to get it checked.'

Later that night, he spoke to my mother, who told him the AC was dry-heaving even when she visited back in October. It is now May.

I know she's told him because he's already on the phone, getting in touch with someone who can come take a look at it the next day, just before he flies home.

Now, he sits across from me and raises a fist in the air and declares, 'BOOKED!' When I acknowledge this with a short smile, he continues to wave the fist around even more determinedly, doing his fatherly duty of pushing the joke to its limit to get that laugh. Something about his cheer roughs up against the inexplicable but routine sadness I've been incubating the whole weekend, and I break down. I can't even place it:

I'm not baking to a light batter-fried crisp for the first time in months, I have a whole weekend of nothing to do ahead of me, I have a job I find meaning in, friends who continually check in on me.

Kind, as always, he sits exactly where is, refusing to make a spectacle of my crying.

'Is it the living-by-yourself?' he asks. I shake my head. I know he really needs to get moving to make his flight on time, and I hate that I had to do this right now. I quickly regain my composure.

'Okay, off you go,' I say to him with a smile.

He hesitantly makes for the door, and as he ties his shoelaces, he asks, 'Why not therapy?'

I don't have anything to say in return, but why not indeed.

'I'm glad I was here to get it fixed,' he says.

'Nanna, I can live without one. That's why I didn't call anyone. It's such a privileged problem.'

'I know you can. It's not about the AC, though, is it?'

He hugs me at the door.

'Can still change your mind and come back home with me forever,' he says dramatically.

I laugh and say, 'I'll keep that as a last resort.'

As I see him disappear down the stairs of the building, I realize what my father meant about the AC. I didn't realize that I 'meant to get around to' something and let it slip by for half a year. I thought I was just lazy, but my father was right—I was mistaking it for a water tanker when it was something else. I was depressed.

How did it come to this? How am I here, a month away from turning thirty, teetering on the edge of the rest of my life, washing the dishes and sobbing over the sink alone?

I call my mother a few minutes later and once I'm all cried out, we dissect all the reasons this could be happening. Seeing my dad only for a day, some kind of hormonal symptom of my PCOS, perhaps a side-effect of my birth control, general homesickness and ennui, mercury retrograde, Nirmal Baba's Third Eye…

'Of course,' she says, rather matter-of-factly, 'you've been working out and eating a low-GI diet for the last ten days. Maybe your body is registering this new change and is in shock. Maybe it thinks you just need carbs.'

Reader, it wasn't the carbs.

I measure the end of things by inanimate objects. A week before Maamma passed away, Varun called her to ask how to make rasam. A few weeks later, after having cremated her, he made the rasam. This is a measure of death. Days after my then-partner left for the US, I noticed the shade of nail polish on my hands that I had put on the day I saw him last. This is a measure of love's loss. I finally get around to watching

Planet Earth, made in 2007, and think of where I was in life then. I hadn't even met my long-term partner then. This is a measure of potentiality. I lose someone's fedora and find it after moving four houses, and four years. This is a measure of kindling. It's an alternative form of auto-ethnography. A form of carbon dating.

The story of loneliness is the story of routine, as if routine is resignation. I remember watching Jennifer Lopez in *The Wedding Planner* when I was in my teens—which starts with a montage of Lopez's character coming home and performing the same routine day in, day out. She comes home, drops her keys, changes into her pyjamas, cooks a microwave dinner and has it in front of her TV—every single night. There are no dialogues to this bit, but the point is lost on no one. It's quickly supposed to establish how mature she is but how lonely and regimented her life has to be because of it. Of course, this wasn't the first movie or the only one to perpetrate this pattern. It's an easy and lazy hack—to show someone living by themselves (especially women) is to show routine. The same bowl, the same plate, the same dinner with the same TV show, the same bedtime routine, as if in the absence of another human being, regimen becomes your spouse. These are women who grew up into responsibilities, even if they were manic pixie girls once. But who talks about the joy, meditation, comforts and liberation of routine?

Month Two at the new job, new city, new house, and it feels like a lifetime. I wake up every day around 7.15 a.m. and make a ritual of the coffee-making process. Move to the espresso machine, store yesterday's coffee grinds in a jar that is food for Rohini's plant growing upstairs, add fresh coffee powder, listen to the machine hiss and sputter the coffee out, and wonder how long it's got before it explodes. Most days, Rohini's around and we chat over morning grogginess and one of us cooks lunch. No matter how much we dilly-dally, though, it's always only 8.45 a.m. Some days, we give up and reach office earlier than expected.

At night, we're each on our own, and I bask in the darkness of my room, which smack-dab faces another house that holds tuition classes for a group of really loud children. Add to it the searing, oppressive heat of the whole city, and my lights are usually off. No matter where I start at the beginning of my sleep, I always end up on the floor, the body craving the kind of coolness that only comes from stone.

I fall into a rhythm during the nights. I come home, quickly eat, and retire for the day into my dark room (which now houses a really small lamp, so I'm not in total darkness). Always a mug or two of non-caffeinated tea. It feels like hours have passed since my trudging home and vegetating, but it'll only be 7.30 p.m. At least three hours to go before the stadium-floodlight-level brightness from the tuition centre opposite my window is turned off and sleep is officially announced.

Some days, I wake up alert at 4.45 a.m., only to see the stadium light back on. The door is open, and the man has started setting up his plastic chair, right in the middle of the room, for optimal vantage point. I shut my paper-thin curtains to block out the light and go back to sleep. When I wake up later, at 6.30 a.m., children are already trudging out of class. Between the exhaustion of 10.30 p.m., when they finish their class, and the grogginess of 5 a.m., I wonder what the textures of their dreams are like.

Over the weekends I meet a bevy of new folks in the city, but it tires me. I do it as some kind of automated necessity because I recognize my world cannot be so insulated—I cannot depend on working, living and hanging out with the same people only. I swipe with half of me already out the door because I'm convinced this is not where I'll find...the thing that I'm supposed to be looking for. I don't know. I've met really kind people, but no one I can see in my own life. I make my peace with the fact that I'm not perhaps looking for anything at all. But this constant moving has exhausted me. This entire decade of upping and moving every two years has perhaps built some slow resentment in me towards moving. Maybe I'm so asocial and given to spending days in my own room (anywhere) because it's the next best thing to digging my nails into a place I know I will be yanked painfully out of. I also build resentment towards it because I take at face value what potential partners have told me over the years—that love is impossible because I cannot/do not stay. Who knows the veracity of such claims? I know, for now, only this:

Attachment is simple. You'll know when it is.

A strange reticence has quietly been overtaking me these last couple of years. I'm aware that I just do not have the energy to share things in detail with folks, and perhaps it started out with the physical separation from life in India and noting that there's no one keeping up with you fully and actively (and it's true of me too). But here I am, a little out of touch with the ones closest to me, because I cannot seem to physically and mentally face up to the question that is often asked of me: How is life? How is everything?

In what language do you tell someone—the one the answer exists in, or the only one that they can hear?

There is a certain loneliness that comes from working towards no longer depending on others for your day-to-day. I hold some resentment towards this necessity of sharpening the blade of independence for years of living alone, and then being too sharp around the edges for any coeval living. You sharpen, sharpen, sharpen yourself until you cannot touch anyone without the risk of hurting them or being hurt yourself. Whenever I move in with new housemates, I do so with all my guards up, my boundaries set in stone. As the weeks pass and I establish a routine, I drop most of these self-censoring rules with the people I live with. For the most part, I am grateful for company, especially company where each of us learns to understand each other. It is calming to hear the sounds of someone else go about their lives, especially when it's a struggle to get out of bed. Every now and then, though, I crumble under the cruelty of these forced intimacies in the absence of desired ones.

After a while, you understand that no matter how much you try fortifying yourself against the storms of a solitary life, you have to build something living and breathing with the people around you. Except, of course, for the tiny fact that building anything takes more than one person, and that leaves you vulnerable to both joy and despair. And because you've fashioned yourself off your distorted reflection in Plato's cave, everything inside seems exaggerated in proportion. On the good days my friends keep me afloat, we're texting each other across cities, continents and time zones constantly. On some other days, the slightest gap in communication becomes a demonstration in catastrophic thinking—someone says something that pisses me off or hurts me, and I scroll my chat window to find someone to vent to, by which time my mind's already decided that everyone in my life is leading a perfectly busy and fulfilled life without me. My accounting shows that it's not just that I don't really have anyone to go to, but if I haven't really noticed, nothing in my life is going particularly well, and might well be on the brink of collapse. *And while we're at it*, my brain bulldozes on, *have you noticed the new unexplained pain you woke up with yesterday? It could be nothing, but what if it's everything you've been anticipating all this while, the last row to connect in your chronic illness bingo? You'll be pinned down at last, so you can be confronted with the fact of your deception, this imposter you've been all your life, taking on the gestures of the place and the people you're with to show you're one of them—but who are you, really?*

The first moments of waking up are perhaps always my most normal. Aches and anxieties haven't kicked in yet and all I feel is that delicious longing to go back to bed—just like everyone else, just like when I was a child. Then, suddenly, in the middle of the day, I am suddenly painfully aware of the present moment, distraught, always, that I am somehow still here, in the driver's seat of this body afforded to me.

As I lie under my covers in bed, on yet another sick day in yet another cityscape, feeling guilty about existing like this at all, some kind of liability to everyone around me—at work, in friendships, in relationships—I think about pushing myself just for today, this one last time, to wake up and eat something, talk to someone, reach out. On my weakest days, the shadows in the cave play up huge, monstrous imagery, and I see myself, an atrophying corpus struggling to hold on to a jittery brain. *How have you done it?* you ask yourself as you pitch your blanket over, around and under you, like a tent. *How did you even make it this far?*

Some days you make a fort and you marvel at it from the inside.

Dating

This is what happens when you live by yourself for a while. In the early days, fresh off the memories of love, but still startling from its abandonment, you think everything is about you. That friend of a friend who has tagged along for a lunch date is there because he heard you're now single. Or maybe the interesting fellow on your friend's email thread is now destined to fall in love with you. You can sense it. The universe owes you one for putting you through an unfair break-up. You take your time meticulously forming your response to the thread. Everyone, but especially that guy, needs to see you're doing fine and are, in fact, not collapsing from heartbreak. By the time you're ready to hit send on the group email, someone's changed the topic, so you abandon ship. Too late to send, too soon to delete. You catch yourself acting this way and feel embarrassed. You see, you still remember what it was like to be loved, the mundane comforts of companionship and what being attractive to someone else felt like. You will conveniently forget what hurt, and anger, and betrayal felt like, but this is the nature of memory. You can never go back to that old space in time, and the only things you can keep with you once the borders to the past are shut are the ones you're never quite sure are not propaganda. Fresh out of a relationship filled with gaslighting and manipulation, all your radars have been compromised. So now anyone who as much as pays you decent attention triggers the alarm signals in your mind: Interest! Interest! Interest! Sometimes someone might even explicitly say they are not interested in anything substantial with you, but your faulty radars are working overtime to show you the real signs and you shake your head in amusement. They can't see that their actions betray their robust love for you. It's like you can't help but look at love in terms of moves—and everyone's making them.

After a few years you fall for some other boy and you love him because of all the ways in which he is not your ex. You both declare your intense, dramatic and effusive love to everyone in your common friend circle, even though they've each told you why this might not work. You can't really tell if you actually like who he is or how he behaves in a relationship, but for this moment it's all you need. His moving to the US is not really a problem for you, because doesn't true love conquer all? Each relationship has its challenges, and this time it is distance, you think. This gives you enough motivation to apply to schools abroad. You move to Vancouver, hoping this might help ease the long distance. It doesn't work; it couldn't work. You mark another humiliating end to another love story. Then you realize there is humiliation because there were witnesses, because you insisted so much on sharing every small detail when you were happy. You decide never to do that again. Everything around you moves as it's used to moving. People break up, but more and more of them get together or get married. You cry some nights, unable to feel joy for anyone in your life who has what you don't. However, this time, the mourning is quicker, easier, and after a few years, you'll have to put in effort to remember this relationship. Life goes on for a while. Then someone from a class you're taking in university suggests a drink at the neighbourhood bar. You look at his text and take a second. You hadn't thought of him in that way before, but could this invitation mean that he is interested in you? You say yes, and spend the rest of the evening deciding what to wear to the bar the next day. Once there, you drink in giddy anticipation until he casually mentions a girlfriend and you sense your body recoiling in shame at your premature delusion—why would anyone be interested in you?

There are at least a few more times in the next two years that you mistake kindness for attraction. Thankfully, each time sobers you up a little more. Slowly, and painfully, you realize that, in fact, nothing is about you. You stop expecting love in new places and with new people, you stop praying for a miracle with the long-familiar people, and somewhere in between a romantic song and watching a movie with couples on every side, you find that you are now unable to imagine a life with someone else. You're taken aback by this realization. *Do I think so lowly of myself?* you wonder, the question humming in the background as you go about your days. But you learn that the inability is just that, an inability to conjure up experiences you don't have any more, and can't for the life of you remember. You think of your father who, never having had a headache in life, asks—like a child, with fleeting wonder and curiosity: *What is it like? What do you feel when you have it? Where exactly does it hurt? And how? Is it like a stomach ache, except in the head?* Yeah, sure, you and your mother say to him, unable to articulate how the one ache is different from the other. You realize you are your father now. *What is it like? What do you feel when you are in companionship? Where exactly does it hurt when you love? Is it like how you love your friends, except nothing like it at all?*

Still, the gospel of a loveless life is devastating. *Burn it all down, there is nothing to salvage here,* you write in a letter to your past self. You mistake epiphany for cure, treatment, release and walk around wanting to advise everyone you know that despite their happiness, you have found out that nothing matters and that everything ends. You want to save them from this pyramid scheme that is romantic love, and who else but you to do this? You who have suffered heartbreak after heartbreak, taking one for the collective hive mind. But the world carries on just fine without your unique discovery. People get together or break up regardless, and you have all this leftover rage and energy from your epiphany that you have to redirect somewhere else, so you try burning down all parts of your life instead.

Whenever you do drink in this new country, you try out different craft beers that the Pacific Northwest has to offer, but all it does is eat into your fellowship money. You suspect your liver and insulin resistance makes your body process alcohol a little slower (faster? differently?) from others, and so the route that takes others to a 'happily buzzed' place your Alcohol GPS skips altogether. It's either being painfully sober all night, even after all that money, or being uncomfortably, unenjoyably drunk, where you remember some things and don't remember others, and you think to yourself that at least that's one more day you've gotten through without being painfully awake. This goes on for days, months—who can keep track of time any more?

You meet your friend Curtis—from your class on War Literature—for drinks and turn up on an empty stomach. Your German friend from precisely two Tinder dates ago also happens to be on campus and you ask him to join you. The whole night, each of the men assume you're probably going to end up with the other, which, at this point, is just a cruel joke but you have to laugh along. Later, you won't understand why you turned up on an empty stomach to a drinking plan, but even if there truly was no intention to this, the forgetting itself is an irresponsibility that is new to you. You remember the first few pints of beer and conversation, and from then on, mostly snatches. At the end of the night, as the bar is closing and everyone's running to catch the last bus out of uni, both men try giving you space to walk homewards with the other. All you remember from then on is crying silently at the bus stop while your Tinder date leaves on a bus and summoning just enough wherewithal to text Curtis and let him know you don't think you can make it home. You ask if you can get some shut-eye at his, just until you're sober enough and a periwinkle dawn cracks through the night sky. Curtis, also drunk, on his part, summons enough wherewithal to come to get you at the bus stop. He notices you're crying and assumes something has happened with the boy from Tinder. As we sit on the 99B line on our way to his place, the tears won't stop rolling. It takes all of Curtis's reserved, dry, thirty-six-year-old white Albertan conditioning to not regret volunteering to get into a sticky emotional situation. He awkwardly pats your shoulder twice, but it only makes you cry harder.

You end up on his couch, walking to and from the bathroom all night, throwing up and trying not to cry loudly. Curtis gives you his warm duvet and sleeps on his bed with a thin, urine-yellow throw with a big hole in it. You would usually feel horrified at this sacrifice, but you're too drunk to care. This is the first time you've visited his house. In fact, you're not even sure you two are good enough friends for him to do you this kind of favour. True to your word, and because even in the middle of a drunken episode, you don't want to come off as a clinger-on, you wake up at the crack of dawn and wait to see if Curtis moves at all, so you can say goodbye. It's not really that you care for social niceties at this hour, but that you don't know how his door locks, so you can slip out quietly. The last thing you want is for Curtis to get robbed because he wanted to help a friend in distress. But he wakes up soon enough and offers to drop you home in his car on his way to work. As you get out of the car, you apologize once again, telling him how embarrassed you are for this behaviour. 'Hey, no problem, we've all been there,' he tells you in his gravelly, monotonous but oddly comforting voice. As kind as he has been, you assume you'll never hear from him again. Surprisingly, maybe because there's nothing better to do, Curtis sticks around. Except whenever you sleep over at his from then on, he sleeps with his duvet. You get the wanking blanket and the couch.

People will keep telling you (always unasked) to 'stay open to the idea of love', whenever you indicate that you're getting better at this being alone, being happy thing. It will prick because they might not understand that you need to jettison a very specific kind of optimism to feel happy with yourself. How can you explain to someone the exhaustion and inefficiency of constantly being open to signs from fate? Good-naturedly, you tell them *oh no no*, you are open, of course. You haven't become a steely automaton. But by this point, you know the hoops you have to jump through to see something through—even if two people are interested in each other. So you don't even know what being 'open' actually means. You are a steely automaton.

They will first say, oh you need to focus on yourself, cultivate some passions outside of yourself, don't go around

hungrily asking/
in the heart's thick accent

for the possibility of love. You have to distract yourself with other hobbies and interests. You take it to heart and try picking a skill to hone. While this is fulfilling in itself, you start noticing that people get together irrespective of whether they have spectacular interests. Then come the gentle suggestions about the few interests you do already have as a 'single feminist'. You will learn that everything you say beyond a certain age is received with judgement. It doesn't matter that you had the same preferences in people at twenty-three as you do now. The only difference is that now your opinion is considered errant at worst or stupid at best because you're single—no other human being has validated you. 'This is why you're not finding men. You're too angry,' I'll hear from one of them, but no one checks to see if that's what I want in the first place.

A boy you meet on Tinder, so beautiful that it's unsettling why he's interested in you, comes over one night to your basement suite. You lay in bed and talk through the night, unsure about where this is all going. You're talking about the symbolism in *Watchmen* when he leans in for a kiss, and you sense some relief, you know where this night is going. Except sex is complicated when you're bleeding half the year and feeling ugly the other half, when not both at the same time. You don't have the bandwidth to explain your PCOS to a stranger, so you quickly turn momentum and focus on his pleasure instead. You make sure he doesn't touch you. He talks to you the rest of the night, telling you things from his childhood that are painful and poignant, and you wonder why he's sharing this trauma and how you're supposed to manage it. He talks and talks till day breaks and you're guilty of being sick of him. You just need a break from soaking all this in. 'I'll see you later?' he asks-says as he leaves, one of my earrings still stuck to his pants. He never gets in touch again, but you hold his trauma safe for him because you hope someone has done the same for you.

In the long periods that you stay off online-dating apps, you lose out on one specific muscle—the one that constantly constructs, updates and recounts the Story of You. Without a vested witness, or the potential of one, you notice that internal stock-taking occurs rarely. You think of the boys you've spoken to online over the years, that specific kind of relationship that isn't strong enough for a name, and drones on only out of inertia and the fear of loneliness until someone either moves on or drains out. You can see your own face, so many weeks, months and years ago, stuck to your phone, the cold, blue light from the screen reflecting in your eyes deep into the night that measures indifferently, as two more people fumble through companionship. The visual catches you off-guard, it makes you think of every relationship you've had and how they've always involved a screen at some point. Relationships either started with long distance or ended in them, because you didn't stay. How poetic, then—you, with your screen, your broken sleep cycle and your constant feeling that you don't even live here. Your heart is always elsewhere. And hasn't this meant that dating someone was necessarily always a kind of loneliness/solitude, and haven't you come to prefer this kind of intimate-but-always-at-a-distance love? Were any of these men even real, you wonder. Did you not just take the rough attributes they offered about themselves on chat and then fill in everything else in your own head? A DIY partner that you either never meet or meet only to realize how different they are, and you part ways. Before you put that thought away, you make a mental note of how a recent book you read referred to certain aspects of online dating as a 'private psychosis'.

That night in July 2016 when you meet a classmate in a neighbourhood bar, you drink with friends even after he leaves. You get home somehow (you've prepared for this all your life, haven't you, with your base routes?) and find a bottle of wine from the last time you hosted dinner for friends. You sit propped against the bed, feeling only two sensations—the thick coir-like carpet under your heels and calves, and the smooth, stone-like coolness of ending it all. It's the clinical, dry nature of this thought in your head that startles you. You get up immediately and open your laptop. One of your closest friends, Jenn, is always up at this hour and she knows you've not been doing too well. You ping her in desperation, 'I don't know why but I feel like I just want to be done with this whole thing.' Jenn responds like she always does, immediately, calmly and kindly. 'Everything is so hopeless, and I just can't get this thought out of my head,' you slur-type. 'I'm here for you,' Jenn says. 'Do I need to call an ambulance?'

Something about what she asks slaps you out of your spiral. 'No, no,' you say, 'just keep talking to me for a bit and I'll be fine.' Slowly, Jenn and you come back down from that crescendo of despair. You'll owe Jenn forever—she understood what little language you had at your disposal to name an ache that seemed unsurmountable, inevitable. The wormhole closes with as much finality as it had opened with.

Everything changes from this moment on. You've been to the brink, looked into the abyss and decided, for whatever it was worth—not now. Not like this. And even though you don't have a problem with drinking, you realize the problematics of drinking in such despair, and you stop. Over the next few months of being sober, you realize it's not even something you particularly enjoyed. You realize if it's just you at the end of the day, if you have to save you, you better get started. Then, after all this, after coming back from the brink of a wildfire that you lit the match to, then, you get a chance at being happy.

You start being kind to yourself.

Planting

When I moved from Vancouver to Chennai in 2017, I was about to turn twenty-nine. By that point I had spent many years by myself, and despite a few crests and troughs, had mostly been single. This would have come as a shock to thirteen-year-old me, who had written a checklist for my twenty-seventh year. I would own a long woollen coat, a perfume that I had paid for myself, have a really 'cool' job and be married. Although I never fantasized about my wedding, or being married to someone, I had assumed that this clinical, administrative milestone would have been covered by then. It was like growing permanent teeth, an automated event in my life. But Year Twenty-Seven had come and passed me by without any promise of romantic fulfilment. I had somewhat made my peace with it, inasmuch as singledom forced this out of you. Marriage was never truly a goal, so that was the first to slip out of my life. Even the desire for long-term commitment soon evaporated, leaving behind a tiny pool of resentment for the fact that in all my life, I was the one who had initiated relationships. I felt defunct. What sort of girl needed to go convince people to date her? While I don't mean to say people dated me out of pity, I held on to the fact that each of my relationships started off with me putting the wheels in motion, turning my personality up so it shone through and they had to take notice. If only those relationships where someone fell for you *first* counted, I used to think, I didn't have any.

As soon as I landed in Chennai, I started meeting a lot of folks off dating apps. This was uncharacteristic for someone like me. All the men I met were sweet, but I entered these dates with one foot out the door at all times. Perhaps it was the depression also catching up with me, maybe the birth control switching my moods, but I soon found myself thoroughly disinterested in going through the motions of first dates and tepid conversations or great conversations and ghosting. What was the point of it all anyway—love was impossible because I knew I would not stay on in Chennai. But I still went on for a bit—swiping and meeting, wanting to prove a point about being proactive. 'Look!' I shouted out into the universe, accusing it of not paying attention, 'I'm putting in effort! What else could you possibly want me to do?'

My friends in Chennai put up a chart in their house with a list of all the people I had been on dates with, so they could keep track. It was part joke, part necessity—the names came and left lunchtime conversations quickly. I remember looking at the chart during lunch once, asking myself why I was doing this at all. Was I genuinely interested in any of them? Were any of them interested in me? The connection I seemed to have with folks from dating apps was that we were in a common predicament. None of us really knew what we wanted any more, except that we maybe, kinda, some days didn't want to be where we were in life and knew this was a thing we had to do. Thoroughly disgusted by how much effort I was putting into something I wasn't even sure I wanted, after three months of whirlwind dating, I deleted all the dating apps. The chart survived for a while longer—it made for great stories. The soil was fertile, and yet nothing grew on it.

Ammama is an expert gardener, a skill neither her first daughter nor her first grand-daughter picked up. Over the years she has tended to and nurtured so many plants and trees in her house in Hyderabad, planting them through and around the concrete so that the house is overtaken by green circuitry. Since she has been living by herself for decades now, the ratio of plants to humans in Lakshmi Kuchibhotla's house is skewed heavily in the former's favour. Through fractures and aches, sickness and anger, Ammama has watered them every day. Even in the ravages of chemotherapy for her terminal ovarian cancer, when the absolute ignominy of being taken care of by her children was forced upon her, she fought to tend to her plants.

When we moved to Mumbai, Ammama visited, in part to say goodbye to me as I left for Vancouver and in part to perform some delicate and literal transplantation. I have a picture of her from then. Her back is facing the camera and she's hunched over a pot. She's in a white cotton saree, crumpled by the goings-on of the day, tending to her bright green saplings against a dull metal sky. I think of how much she looks like Amma, especially as both of them grow older, skin slipping off their shrinking shoulders, hanging like a loose T-shirt. She sat for a while, tending to each pot, planting the sapling, patting the soil, telling Amma how much water and sunlight each of them needed. These are the two things I hold closest to me when I think of her. That even in the midst of cancer, in the envelope of death and devastation, her touch soothed the things she loved. What a legacy to have, to nurture things, to keep them alive.

Before leaving for Vancouver, Amma and I went to buy a pressure cooker for me to take there. We asked for the smallest one the shop had, and I packed with me a tiny bonzai 0.5-litre steel cooker. I had lived by myself before this, but it was the first thing I owned that was tailored to one person, just me.

My housemate in Vancouver, Idalia, and I would cook separately, and it was freeing to not have to worry about anyone else but my appetite and my preferences. Like it was in Pune, like it would be in Chennai, Vancouver, too, was already 'set up' for me. The landlords had provided everything, down to the last spoon, cup and towel. One day, while grocery-shopping together, Idalia and I found the tiniest egg pans and bought one each with different-coloured handles. It was just a pan, just a silicone handle, but it was thrilling to have a small piece of ourselves in the kitchen, fit to our portion sizes and personalities in the midst of all that otherness. When I passingly complained about having had a distinct lack of personal style all my life, my friend Mary reminded me that style often necessitated the luxury of being still, of living in your own space. Utensils might not really be the first things you associate with someone's personal style or taste, but they became the epicentre of all changes in my life. A small pressure cooker, a tiny pan, a soup bowl, an espresso cup.

I carried that habit with me to Chennai. After almost a year of living there, when I finally felt like I might, after all, live there, I bought utensils for one. Like previous houses, this one already came with things in place, so I bought only when something needed replacing. At first I felt silly buying something that tiny when I had a roommate (even though Rohini and I hardly ate the same things for dinner), when I was a member of society. How would I manage in case anyone came home for dinner or when my parents came to stay? But how many people had come and stayed with me, or how many people had I invited to dinner in Chennai that required me to cook all meals? If friends did come over, I decided, I would take it as it comes. But that almost never happened. It's just me, like it's been.

Nearly a year later, I walked into my kitchen one early morning and looked at my thimble-sized south Indian coffee filter, my small milk pot, a pan the size of a notebook, and thought for a second that I had entered Ammama's kitchen. I had wanted her kitchen ever since I was a child. Most utensils could hold portions for one or two people and I loved how cute they looked. There is something affirming about having objects tailored to one's needs. I was living by myself and the utensils I used every day and the food I cooked in it reflected that.

For many months in Chennai, I put in effort only in cooking lunches, because they were shared in office. My other two meals would be whatever was easiest to reach. Anything that was not convenient or cooked/reheated in two minutes seemed a bit precious. I can't place a finger on when I started cooking proper meals for myself, but I'm sure it came hand-in-hand with my deteriorating gut health. I couldn't move out of the house without feeling sick to my stomach, worrying about having to run to the bathroom. A routine trip to a friend's house would be anxiety-ridden, all paths measured in units of restrooms. How many accessible restrooms away was a certain place?

I had a particularly horrible flight from Goa to Chennai, in which I had to pop all the stomach-upset-related pills I carry on me, praying I wouldn't pass out with the discomfort and pain. In mid-air, through particularly bad turbulence, I closed my eyes and wished that someone was there with me, so I could just pass out—I would then be their problem. I was so, so tired. I survived the flight without anything severe happening and made my way to office, drained. On the way, I remembered how Idalia and I would often joke about doing the dishes. 'We cook like someone else is going to come wash the dishes!' we'd groan, hands on hips, trying to assess how it was that dishes performed some kind of cell division in a sink, multiplying overnight. I realize I had been living all this while as if someone else was going to come and care for me.

Why do we think we are not deserving of things when we are alone? I don't mean self-indulgence, I've bought myself enough things, ordered in food to satiate my cravings or to celebrate the weekend. Why don't we feel deserving of effort or discipline? Even after that epiphany on the Goa flight, it took many months for me to start having the energy to cook for myself. Maybe there's something sad and lonely about cooking an elaborate meal for one. You keep thinking to yourself, with some self-pity, 'Oh please! Who'll make all that effort just for silly old me?' One day, your desire for a particular home-cooked meal overtakes your laziness and you cook a wholesome meal for yourself and eat it at the table. There's still a nasal voice in my head that repeats the question, 'Ehhh, who's going to take all that effort the next time?' And I answer: *Me. Me. That's who.*

We need a word for something that is neither 'happiness' nor 'depression' but somehow also both. Something that means 'I am grateful for where I am and feel a strength knocking through my bones, signalling to me that it has my back, but I also feel these other things, as urgently, as sensorially'. At twenty-eight, it's a feeling I carry in the webbings of my fingers. I struggle with it on Mondays in particular, when most of Vancouver checks in on one another, wanting to know how the weekend has been.

Absolute strangers will smile and ask, 'Hey, how's it going?', and the response is usually immediate, seamless, 'Good, how about you?' A quick dance performed all across the city, on buses, on sidewalks, at the cashier's till, in classrooms when you run into old acquaintances.

When I first came to Canada, I didn't realize the finesse and acumen involved in this exchange. It took me months to learn the timing of this verbal choreography, looking on in wonder as a friend I was walking with performed the moves with someone else walking in the other direction, without missing a step. A quick nod, a casual toss of the head. The fluidity of this verbal volley was never mine. Eighteen months later, I am still fumbling. Not used to using words in place of other words, I pause too long to collect all my truths into the judicious brilliance of 'Great! How about you?', managing only to sputter 'Good, good' and smile at the person instead, hoping this social nicety will make up for my baffling incompetence at the other.

As the checkpoints for every year keep passing me by—long-term relationship, career vision, international vacations, marriage, financial security, etc.—I've grown to desire that elusive word even more. I write on a tissue paper: *'I'll tell you what living alone is like: It is like signing up for Zumba classes and telling everyone about it, then bailing on it midway and crafting a wonderful excuse for those who will definitely ask—but no one ever does.'*

So much of my discomfort with being single has come not from a desire for romance or sex, but a vested witness. On most days I feel like this life can go on forever—me in grad school, living alone, on my own, a fleeting community of friends, colleagues and lovers. Other moments I find myself cancelling plans because it grates me that everyone else in the group is bringing someone along with them. Somewhere between those two sentiments, the word slips in quietly. Well-meaning friends ask me about my 'love life', and rush to assure me it will all work out when I tell them I don't have one. Somewhere between the habit of solitude and the catharsis of community in a foreign country, I realize I am no longer looking. Instead, I look around at all the intimacy I do have with friends across the world. I recognize the twenty-odd people I can diffuse my energies into, instead of depending on just the one. And just as there are ways in which the one partner cannot equal twenty friends, the opposite is also true. Between these two truths, the word quietly moves in.

We need that word. For when I realize that I am susceptible to feeling impenetrable wherever I am in the world and that 'home' is whatever I can pack and customs can clear. For when you use the word 'single' to imply the current fact of your life, not the desire to end it. But also for the endless nights when your family in that time zone is too busy, your friends in this time zone are asleep and the Internet won't refresh fast enough to keep up with your loneliness. For missing things without always wanting them. For asking the universe to leave you alone and then not knowing what to do when it gives you just that. For friends who leave me food in my fridge as an amulet for the days I cannot bring myself to do anything. For friends who say 'I'm sorry you had to go through that' or 'Not acceptable! Only the best for you!'. For those who persist through the white noise of long distance and time zones, others who insist on making plans that I wish I don't say yes to, until they actually happen. For friends who send me postcards from places in the world I haven't visited, making me part of their discovery. Those who leave me balloons for when I travel across the world and return to my room, remember that I am allergic to eggs or that I like Hoyne's Dark Matter. For those who invite me home for Christmas dinner and share their family, for those who are only a car ride away, who are outside my door waiting by the time I have texted them about illness, despair or rage. For those who host me in a different country, for those who remind me to 'Do it afraid'. For these wonderful, nurturing friendships with men and women that are deep but weightless, free from the burden of romantic possibility. For those who think it's simply unacceptable that I've gone this long in life without having had pho, sushi, Ethiopian, Yemeni or Korean food. Who do the dishes while I cook, while we sip wine and talk about things far away—now borders, now Sylvia Wynter and how to contain the ever-expanding cosmos in our tiny beating hearts. A word for this buoyant constellation that rushes to keep each other afloat, even as we are individually drowning.

So when they ask me how I'm doing, especially on Mondays, I balance this inarticulable sentiment with an unknowable one:

'Oh, you know...'

And they do.

There are two seasons to Vancouver: Rain and the threat of it. When I first arrived, it poured for days. I quickly learnt that I was going to have to buy sturdy rain boots and a few types of umbrellas, and it wasn't until I bought my windproof one that my membership as a Vancouverite activated. I watched, for days, through the screens of many bus windows, the towering thickets of pine, a fleeting picture show that looped an endless blur of deep greens, pale blues, grainy greys—the official colours of the Pacific Northwest.

For the first few months, I sleep with the lights on in my rental basement suite. I'm not alone, I have a housemate whom the stars have matched for me—both of us quiet, asocial and chatty only in spurts. Still, the silence of a house in the West is nothing like I've experienced in all my life back in India. At first, though, I don't understand why sleep is unsettling, and chalk it up to an unfamiliar environment. As a previously lifelong fan of all things horror, I am forced to jettison the pleasure of fear in Vancouver. When my housemate and my landlords aren't in town, I stop listening to anything that might be unsettling. Podcasts, movies, Reddit threads. For a few nights in my basement, I think I hear idle footsteps outside my window in the middle of the night. I am now used to the sound patterns of the house, and these are new. I sleep with a knife on my bedside table one night. The next morning, I sheepishly confess to Idalia that I may have overreacted by keeping a kitchen knife within my reach, and to my surprise, she reveals she did the same. Later, we find out from our landlords that their daughter is home from college, and Idalia and I realize it was probably her, coming back from a dinner or a party. We feel silly about yesterday's fear, and chuckle to ourselves. The knives are always kept within reach, regardless.

The neighbourhood I live in is clearly rich, and almost entirely white, except for women of colour who work as nannies. My block in particular is beautiful, manicured lawns, coloured doors, beautiful ornamental trees lining the streets. But almost half the houses are empty; my landlords tell me they're probably vacation homes for people living outside the country. By night, therefore, the block looks deserted, dark, except for a flicker of habitation here and there. This isn't as scary as I had feared—I walk back with enough confidence even after a night out, taking the night bus back at 2 a.m. But there's something insidious about the absolute stillness of my surroundings, and it slowly deposits on to my bones, until being unsettled comes from deep within me. Transplanting to an environment where you might not see another human for miles, or where you're the only brown person to enter the room, is oddly affecting. I arrive in fall, and before I can marvel at the pumpkin-yellow, golden-orange, wine-red hues of Vancouver, winter unfurls. The basement suite doesn't get enough natural light even in the peak of summer, so my room light is always on, an endless day, an endless night. If there's no class that day, I lose track of time easily; everything is tinged with the same fluorescent orange. It isn't until I travel to Atlanta for a conference, until I sleep in the guest bedroom in my friend Isha's house, until I hear cars whoosh by late into the night outside the house, until I get the best sleep of my life, that I realize how silent it is back in my basement. I also learn, at the same time, how wood speaks. The house groans and heaves, the floorboards expand and contract, there are always strange noises. One day, I nap a little too hard in the evening and forget to switch on the lights in my room. I start switching the lights off eight months after moving in.

Within the narrow grids of the city that I traverse, I make friends and slip into communities quickly. Even in my quiet neighbourhood, everyone smiles or nods as we cross one another. I enjoy this polite volley, this looking a stranger in the eye and wishing them a good day, offering a cursory smile. This is the precise amount of interaction I need to feel alive and engaged. My master's programme in Gender, Race, Sexuality and Social Justice is also particularly unique in that it necessitates that we all work with a mindfulness and emotional quotient way more demanding than any other course. All of us live our theories, so our classroom discussions and lectures often border on raw, livewire collective therapy. Some days I am desirous of such a catharsis, of being heard and witnessed by my classmates. Other days we're all exhausted by the constant extraction of our emotions. I try doing what I learnt in my literature class—I try finding the switch, so I can turn it off, just for a second. But it doesn't work here. However, I have never felt more at home than with the people I have become friends with at UBC. Very quickly we form intimate friendships, and are a large sentient organism, with everyone somehow flexing the same muscles of empathy and resilience. It takes my GRSJ programme for me to realize that I have never truly felt this at home before. For once, I am not an embedded reporter filing my notes about the community I'm living in. These are my people, I'm part of this community.

In all of this, still, a dissonance accumulates. I seem to be living a life that fits my worldview perfectly, but it is also incredibly isolating. Even for someone who isn't given to physical expressions of love or friendship, the physical isolation of the West becomes unbearable. Without the sensation of touch, I might as well be a simulation or superimposed on to a green screen. How can I tell if I'm really here, in this house, in this city? In the middle of hanging out with friends, I am overcome with the compulsion to reach out and touch them. The first semester in UBC I am excited, happy to talk about the country I'm from whenever someone asks. By the second semester, I start tiring of being expected to contextualize India in discussions. I start putting a disclaimer at the beginning or the end of my interjections, 'There are many Indias, and I can only speak from my extremely privileged experience of it.' By the third semester, I wonder if anyone can even tell the difference if I just lie. I'm often the only brown person, or Indian, in a classroom and there's no one around to check me. I don't lie, but I stop offering contextualizations in discussions. I speak, like my Canadian or American classmates do, as if everyone just knows what is happening in India. That people's reactions or interactions in discussions don't change either way surprises me.

But there is also another truth swirling in the background: Up until I stepped out of the country, I held on to the fact that I was Indian. Through all the moving across the decades, I was still very much within the constructed borders of one country. There was still some semblance of identity. But when I'm sitting in a classroom and talking about the country, I realize I don't really belong to any one city or culture. I can't speak with any true authorial expertise on anything. In revealing myself, I am revealed. I register this unmooring of identity.

I apply for a PhD in Literature at my university, get a conditional offer and refuse. The calculus for what I'm giving up in Vancouver to hold on to in India has been performed. I choose the risk of *this* unhappiness over *that*. I book my tickets for home.

Somewhere in the last semester of my programme, I read in a book by Beverly Nichols, 'It is ridiculous to rent things if you are a gardener; it fidgets you. Even a very long lease is upsetting. I once owned a house with a 999-year lease and it gave me an unbearable sense of being a sort of week-end guest; it hardly seemed worthwhile planting the hyacinths.' This is exactly what I do—the inverse of hoarding. Owning things gives me so much anxiety that I try not buying anything. From the day I move into a new space, I'm preparing to leave by trying to stay light. Across all the years of moving, I build a compulsion to let go. It creeps into my digital life too. I don't bother about transferring pictures from an old phone to a new one. Holding on is excruciating—it is attachment, and attachment is painful. I want to be light, light, light. But I see friends and classmates around me who are living through stories of displacement, dispossession, countries that have been ravaged by proxy wars. I learn the importance of resilience. I can be as heavy as I want. Heaviness is okay, heaviness is safe.

I realize the conundrum my subconscious insists on: I have to be light, I cannot be too light.

A chance meeting with an older queer man in Atlanta at an academic conference turns into an intimate friendship, bursting at the seams. He offers to take me to the best taco place in town before I leave and asks me to meet him at a nearby coffee shop so he can pick me up. My friend Isha is amused but supportive. 'Just keep me in the loop, and keep texting.' It's the first time I don't look at a map, to trick my mind into thinking I 'know' this place. I don't know this place. I walk to the coffee shop, feeling a flash of giddiness as I trot along the crosswalk. Look at me, doing this. Over the best tacos (indeed), we discuss mortality and grieving, both public and personal. Somewhere in the middle of that raw conversation, Edward gifts me a phrase that will change a lot in the course of my life. The phrase comes from a friend of his, but he is generous with this gnostic wisdom. I tell him about how I've stopped reading into chance encounters or hoping for them. 'Post-narrative world,' he tells me. 'You're living in a post-narrative world, free from the burden of living a story, of being one.' Into each life some rain must fall, but there is no guarantee that romantic love will too. Edward and I both know this might be the last time we meet in person; we nurture what we have precisely for the moments we have it, and then say our goodbyes. On my flight back to Vancouver, I roll the phrase inside my head. Post-narrative world. That's where I am. There's no right place to be, or to have been by now, because even though Tiny Shruti sitting next to her mother swaying over a picture book will always look for The Story, I now learn that for someone like me, it's the life without the anticipation of one where I can be agile. I sit with the phrase over the next few days, weeks, months. Oh, to be light again.

We're spending Christmas at Noal and Adam's, creating our own little holiday tradition. Noal has gifts for each of us. Taq's here with her partner, Iman's here with her sister, also my friend, Anwaar, and there are moments when I am slightly envious of everyone having someone to go back home with. No one's actually making me feel like this, this is all a projection. But because I'm still learning the ropes of the post-narrative life, an old, familiar ache pops up sulkily as I look at everyone around the room. *And who do you have?*

I blink the sudden threat of tears away. Later that night, just as we're all about to leave, Noal and Adam bring out gifts, individually wrapped for each of us. They go around the room, as Taq, her partner, Iman and Anwaar open their presents. When it's my turn, I see that Noal and Adam each have something for me. I get two. And, of course, it is not about the number, but it also is. Their act of love is small, but Noal and Adam lay the foundation for something much larger that night. I needn't spend my life's anxieties agonizing over stories that aren't yet formed, that will perhaps never form; I'll always have stories tucked away within these smaller acts of love. *I'll always have me.*

I portion the love for and knowledge of my friends in different parts of my room, sectioning and siphoning off things I want them to have once I'm gone. All the things in the pantry for

Iman and Noal, some books for Rachel and Jenn, clothes that Leah and Kaye might like, rain boots for Anwaar, my new Crockpot for Sampath. I want them to remember me by, but like the memory of our times together, mostly through perishable items. And so I burrow, and my friends absorb parts of me in the things I leave behind.

Abeer, a friend of mine who works for a radio station, asks me to record something for an in-house advertisement on my way out from a radio interview. In it I'm asked to say one or two things I associate with Vancouver so that it leads up to 'Vancouver, to me, is XYZ Radio'. I haven't prepared anything beforehand, so I ask the producer for a second to collect my thoughts. I know what I want to say already, always, but the commercial is only a couple of seconds, so I need to be both precise and articulate. I record my statement and am told it'll start being aired in a couple of weeks. On my way back home, I realize I'll have left the country for India by the time. My voice will continue being played on air in my city, the one I have chosen not to overstay my welcome in, long after I will leave it. This is a measure of weight. I was here briefly and it mattered.

March in Vancouver is an explosion of pastel pink and powdery white, emerald green branches pencilled against a sunny clear cloudless blue sky. The cameras are out, open-toed footwear is a thing again, and everyone is filled with joy. I almost missed my first spring in Vancouver because I travelled to Atlanta for a conference before going to India for the summer. This meant that I missed Vancouver's famous cherry blossoms. I had made the mistake of assuming they'd still be in bloom when I was back (and this should show you how pitiful my knowledge of plants is in general). But the cherry blossoms bloom almost overnight, and stay only for a few weeks, if that.

The next year, since I'm in the city, I take a walk down my neighbourhood. One of the streets has cherry blossom trees on both sides of it, so when it comes to bloom, the street is transformed into a stunning canopy. This is magical to me. The same route you pass through every day is now something else altogether. For the first time in a long time, I don't pull my phone out for pictures. I tuck it firmly back into my pocket and look up instead. I can't help but let my jaw hang loose in awe, and I see the odd tourist with their camera do the same. I don't know what it is about that exact moment in my life, and perhaps it is because of the circumstances of that exact moment in my life, that the cherry blossoms stand in for something else: the passage of time, the ephemerality of it. Here we both were, the cherry blossom flower and I, alien and temporary to the landscape, capable of generating (the blossom) and experiencing (me) so much joy. It is here that I feel both grounded and weightless in measures that feel right.

I learn much later that the cherry blossom trees were a gift from Japan to the city of Vancouver in the 1950s as commemoration, an eternal memory of friendship. Over the next decade, the city administration realized that these were preferable to the larger elms, maples and other huge trees, because their roots didn't cause damage to the underground sewers and pavements. Strong enough to stay a while, light enough to leave no trace. I obsess over the idea of tattooing the flower on me, in honour of everything the city has given me and has been witness to. Tellingly, the feeling stays a while before it goes.

I write in my diary later: *Some days I feel like all I am is a weightless cherry blossom with a preternatural sense for rain.*

Two months before my anchor breaks and I am to leave this city, I put up a string of photographs in my room and get myself bathroom scales, a Crockpot, a pack of 150 tea bags, a membership card to Shoppers with the knowledge that each of these things will outlive my time in Vancouver. Two months before my anchor breaks, I plant my hyacinths.

There are two seasons to everything: change and the threat of it.

Acknowledgements

Who really owns a story? How much of a common experience is mine to claim? How many people own jurisdiction over an experience outside of one's head?

As tempting as it was to write this memoir as if it were a tell-all, this is decidedly not *that* book. The story I'm threading together is done so with deliberation and some amount of poetic licence. It is an offering, a guided stop-motion-picture tour of rootlessness, chronic illness and solitude. This is but a selective reading of my life, and perhaps from the one person who'd be most biased about it—me. I am remembering and writing about things that actually did happen, but I believe that remembering is itself a narratorial act. In the act of writing this book, I've had to rake through my whole life, and what I found was this: We remember, mostly, the things we want to, and in the case that a not-so-nice memory overstays its welcome, we make our peace by remembering it in the way we want to. This is why, in the rare instances that some names do appear, especially from my childhood, they have been changed on purpose. I cannot assume that these associations are always welcome. Since this is a book about my life, and I have always needed writing to process my world, in a sense, without my knowing, I've always been writing this book. There were so many recurring themes or topics, flotsam jetsam that I wanted to work on but they never seemed complete or whole. As the years went by, I had a folder of things that didn't fit in anywhere else, but they all fit in together. This is that book.

I have, over the course of my life, been blessed to be part of a quivering collective that I'd like to thank, because, in a way, these stories are eventually theirs too.

My editors at Rupa, for seeing heft where even I didn't, and thus, persisting.

To Asha, Shalini, Isha and Girish, who, in the absence of childhood friends, filled up that hole in my life so sincerely and seamlessly. I hold on to your continued presence in my life with wonder and gratitude.

Swetha, I remember asking you when we were nineteen and I was in love, to remind me that this feeling could exist whenever I felt all was lost. For holding me up to that standard, always, and for holding me up in general.

Devika, Sriti, Cletus, Tanvi, Pradeep, Nitin and Arpita, I am constantly moved by your unwavering support and encouragement. To Karthik, for opening up my world, and to Shodhan, for you know what.

To Rohini, Ragini, Dhwani and Josi, for making Chennai home.

Curtis and Jenn, lighthouses in an alien country, always welcoming, always just an emergency text away from pulling up at my front door with the promise of escape. And, somehow, doing it even now, 12,000 kilometres apart.

Noal, Adam, Iman, Anwaar, Sampath, Rachel, Kristi, Kaye, Conor, Victoria, Leah, Pedro and Camille—where would I have been in life without your continued kindness, humour, strength and insight? Thank you for folding me into your lives. To Edward, Maddie, Sheila, Manny, Khaldah and Lauren, for bringing me so much joy in such a short time—I wish we had more time together.

To my fantastic mentors—Sanam Khanna, Abantika Banerjee, V. Geetha, Gita Wolf and Judy Segal—for their rigour and guidance. To Dina Alkassim, who reminded me that a life without truth and heft would only take me so far.

Inayat, for the many irreplaceable things you've brought to my life, but especially the gift of witness. Harshita, Sasha and Priya, for your unparalleled critical and empathetic eye, steadying me through it all.

My first chosen family—Shweta, Suraj, Veda, Ahana, Jahnavi and Janice—who give me laughter and belonging. And to Mrunmayi, shining your light on us still, forever young. To everyone else, especially my family, for weathering the white noise of my routine absences, and with magnanimity, loving me just the same.

To little Varun in the orange sweater and booties, who

placed his tiny hand on my cheek and knighted me capable of the most expansive love at the age of four.

And, to Aditya, for typhooning into my world not so long ago, making it suddenly awash with unbearable and irreplaceable lightness.

Made in the USA
Monee, IL
03 May 2026